Student Almanac of African American History

Volume 2: From Reconstruction to Today,

1877–Present

Student Almanac of African American History

Volume 2: From Reconstruction to Today, 1877–Present

GREENWOOD PRESS

Westport, Connecticut • London

Library of Congress Cataloging-in-Publication Data
Media Projects, Inc.
Student almanac of African American history.
 p. cm—(Middle school reference)
 Includes bibliographical references and index.
ISBN: 0–313–32596–0 (set: alk. paper)—ISBN: 0–313–32597–9 (v. 1)—
ISBN: 0–313–32598–7 (v. 2)
 1. African Americans—History—Miscellanea—Juvenile literature. 2. African
Americans—History—Sources—Juvenile literature. 3. Almanacs, American—Juvenile
literature. I. Series.
E185.S897 2003
973'.0496073—dc21   2002035332

British Library Cataloguing in Publication Data is available.

Copyright © 2003 by Greenwood Publishing Group, Inc.

Library of Congress Catalog Card Number: 2002035332

ISBN: 0–313–32596–0 (set)
   0–313–32597–9 (vol. 1)
   0–313–32598–7 (vol. 2)

First published in 2003

Greenwood Press, 88 Post Road West, Westport, CT 06881
An imprint of Greenwood Publishing Group, Inc.
www.greenwood.com

Printed in the United States of America

The paper used in this book complies with the
Permanent Paper Standard issued by the National
Information Standards Organization (Z39.48–1984).

10 9 8 7 6 5 4 3 2 1

A Media Projects, Inc. Production
Contributing Writers: Helene Avraham, Beverly Vallencourt, Carolyn Jackson
Design: Amy Henderson
Production: Anthony Galante and Jim Burmester
Editors: Helene Avraham and Carter Smith
Copy Editor: Beth Wilson
Indexer: Marilyn Flaig

CONTENTS

Volume 2: From Reconstruction to Today, 1877–Present

From Reconstruction to Today
1877–Present

"I have a dream that one day this nation will rise up and live out the true meaning of its creed: 'We hold these truths to be self-evident: that all men are created equal.' . . . I have a dream that my four children will one day live in a nation where they will not be judged by the color of their skin but by the content of their character. I have a dream today."

–Dr. Martin Luther King, Jr.

In 1877, the era known as **Reconstruction** (see Vol. 1, p. 123) came to an end. Federal troops, sent to the South to enforce the new laws that were meant to give former enslaved African Americans new rights, packed their bags and went home. When they left, African Americans in the South found that once again, they were prevented from voting. Nor could they send their children to schools that would give them a proper education. Worse still, they found that if they tried to vote or spoke up for the rights that the **Civil War** (see Vol. 1, p. 108) was supposed to have won them, they often became the victims of violence and murder at the hands of white mobs. It would take many years for this situation to change. While the Union had been saved from breaking in two, in many ways it remained a divided nation—one white, and one black. It is those years, and the struggle to complete the battle for freedom for all Americans that Volume 2 of the *Student Almanac of African American History* is about.

THE LATE 19TH CENTURY

The first chapter of this volume covers the years between 1877 and 1896. When Reconstruction ended, some former slaves left the South and headed west to settle in Kansas, Oklahoma or elsewhere (see **Exodusters**, p. 22). However, most others continued to live in the South, sometimes on the same plantations that they had worked on as slaves. They worked as **sharecroppers** (see p. 29), keeping a share of the crops they grew for themselves in return for use of the land. The sharecropper's life was hard. They usually needed to borrow from the landowner to obtain tools and other supplies. In this way, they usually found themselves deeply in debt.

Many local governments also passed laws that kept African Americans separated from the rest of society. For example, African Americans had to ride in separate cars on trains, go to separate schools, eat in separate restaurants, and shop in separate stores from white people. These laws were known as **Jim Crow Laws** (see p. 24). In 1896, the Supreme Court ruled in *Plessy v. Ferguson* (see p. 26) that Jim Crow laws were legal, as long as the facilities provided to blacks were "separate but equal." Although facilities for African Americans were not equal to those for whites, this court case helped enforce segregation for the next 50 years.

BOOKER T. WASHINGTON AND W. E. B. DU BOIS

In Chapter 1, readers will also find information about two of the most important leaders in African American history. **Booker T. Washington** (see p. 32), founder of the Tuskegee Institute believed that the best way for African Americans to improve their lives was to work hard and learn practical skills. **W. E. B. Du Bois** (*doo-BWA*) (see p. 53) disagreed. Du Bois believed that African Americans needed more than practical skills. He wrote that the most talented of them needed to educate themselves to stand up for African American rights and not settle for less than that to which every American was entitled. In Chapter 2 of this book, readers will find information on Du

Bois and the **National Association for the Advancement of Colored People (NAACP)** (see p. 62), which he helped to found in 1909.

THE HARLEM RENAISSANCE

During the early 20th century, many African Americans decided to leave the South to build new lives in northern cities, such as Chicago, Detroit, and New York. When the United States entered **World War I** (see p. 67) in 1917, many African Americans were able to find work in weapons factories.

By the 1920s New York's Harlem neighborhood had become the center of African American art, literature, and music. This blossoming of talent became known as the **Harlem Renaissance** (see p. 67). Musicians like Duke Ellington, writers like Langston Hughes, and artists such as Augusta Savage brought new attention and respect to African Americans.

The long struggle for rights continued as the United States headed into **World War II** (see p. 67). Early in the war, African Americans found that many defense industry factories refused to hire them. Readers will learn how labor leader A. Philip Randolph helped change this, by threatening to lead a protest march on Washington. Also you'll learn how African Americans in the military protested against discrimination in the ranks. You'll read how they showed their heroism in battle.

THE CIVIL RIGHTS MOVEMENT

Chapter 3 of this volume covers the period sometimes known as the "civil rights years." During this period, which lasted from 1946 to 1968, the struggle for equality took center stage. First, in 1946, major league baseball became integrated, as **Jackie Robinson** (see p. 91) joined the Brooklyn Dodgers. In 1954, the Supreme Court overturned the *Plessy* v. *Ferguson* decision by declaring that forced segregation was illegal since separate facilities could not be equal. In the case of ***Brown v. Board of Education*** (see p. 81), the Court declared that it was no longer legal for African American children to be banned from going to school with white students.

Despite these victories, the main battles of the civil rights years were still to come. Although the Supreme Court said segregation was illegal, many still fought against integration. When a woman named Rosa Parks refused to move to the "colored section" of a bus in Montgomery, Alabama, one day in 1955, she set in motion a decade of conflict between those who still wanted to enforce Jim Crow laws and those who felt the time had come for change. In this chapter, **Martin Luther King Jr.**'s (see p. 84) work to bring change through nonviolent resistance is covered. So too is **Malcolm X** (see p. 87), the **Nation of Islam** (see p. 61) leader who argued that African Americans had every right to defend themselves, by "any means necessary."

AFRICAN AMERICA TODAY

Sadly, both Malcolm X and Martin Luther King, Jr. were assassinated before the 1960s came to an end. Because of their work and the work of those who have followed them, African Americans have won many victories. In Chapter 4, you'll read how African Americans have won election to office throughout the nation, and have served in the highest levels of the national government. African American businesspeople have become role models for all Americans. Artists, writers and entertainers have changed American culture. Although there remain many challenges ahead, the story of African American history is a story of success. The next chapters of this story are yours to write.

HOW TO USE THIS BOOK

Each chapter in *Student Almanac of African American History* is composed of two parts. The first part is a short essay that gives a summary of the major events in that time in African American history. The second part is an A–Z section that describes many important people, events, and terms that have to do with the time period.

To help readers find related ideas more easily, many terms are cross-indexed. Within both the essay and A–Z section of each chapter, some words appear in **bold letters**, followed by a page number. That means the term is also a separate A–Z entry in the book which should be read for more information. Other unfamiliar words are printed in ***bold italics***. Short definitions of these words can be found in a glossary that begins on page 127. Finally, words that may be hard to pronounce are followed by a pronunciation key.

CHAPTER ONE

Separate But Equal

The Late 19th Century, 1877-1896

"Negroes did not surrender the ballot easily or immediately. They continued to hold remnants of political power in [seven southern states]. Black Congressmen came out of the South until 1895 and black legislators served as late as 1896. But it was a losing battle, with public opinion, industry, wealth and religion against them."

—W.E.B. Du Bois

In the years between the end of **Reconstruction** (see Vol. 1, p. 123) and the beginning of the 20th century there were new hardships for African Americans. Slavery had been destroyed, but the United States still had not made life safe for African Americans. African Americans still struggled for equality with whites. In numerous instances, African Americans were terrorized by midnight strikes and **lynchings** (see p. 25).

A FATEFUL ELECTION

The controversial presidential **election of 1876** (see p. 22) ended the **Reconstruction** era (see Vol. 1, p. 123). Democrat Samuel Tilden won the popular vote over Republican Rutherford B. Hayes. However, 20 *electoral votes* were in question. A special group was appointed to study the matter. The election was awarded to Hayes. White voters in the South threatened to *secede* again from the Union. So, Hayes offered a deal. He would remove the remaining federal troops from the South. Those troops were there to ensure that African Americans would be treated fairly.

This was a blow to African Americans. The Republican Party had been **Abraham Lincoln**'s (see Vol. 1, pp. 85, 119) party. Although not all

Republicans had favored the end of slavery, most **abolitionists** (see Vol. 1, pp. 45, 73) had been Republicans. After the **Civil War** (see Vol. 1, p. 108), Republicans dominated the government. Some of the party's members, called "Radical Republicans," had passed laws to ensure that freedmen were allowed to take part in government. Most Republicans in the South were African Americans. A conservative mood had come over Republicans in the North. They were now more interested in the welfare of business than the welfare of African Americans.

The Democratic Party had supported slavery before the war. In Reconstruction, it favored whites. By 1876, the party had regained control of the South. Democrats became the majority party in all the states under Reconstruction. Still, African American men held office and participated in public life. No women of any race could vote or hold office.

ECONOMIC PROBLEMS ABOUND

When the Civil War ended, the economies of the North and West boomed with the growth of the railroads. Businessmen made risky financial investments. Many politicians passed laws that encouraged and aided this practice. During this era, many politicians and government officials took payoffs and bribes from businesses. Writers Mark Twain and Charles Dudley Warner used the phrase "the gilded age" to describe this time. The word "gilded" means covered with a thin layer of gold. However, underneath this thin layer of "gold,"

Timeline

1866

The first African American army regiments, nicknamed **Buffalo Soldiers**, are formed.

1873

After a panic in the stock market, an economic depression begins.

the U.S. economy was rotting. In 1873, a panic in the stock market brought more than a decade of hard times to all regions of the United States.

In the South, nearly everyone suffered economically. African Americans suffered most. The war had greatly damaged the region's farmland, cities and railroads. Plantation owners had lost their work force. When they tried to convince former enslaved peoples to work in gangs on contract, they refused. Now owners came up with a new plan. They would divide their land into portions, or shares. Workers who lived on them could keep half the crop. This arrangement, called **sharecropping** (see p. 29), was attractive to both poor African Americans and whites. The idea was that they could earn enough money to buy land of their own. In reality, sharecropping kept them in debt. The money they borrowed in order to plant crops was never paid off. Often, the landowner ran a store that supplied the sharecropper with credit for food and supplies. Most sharecroppers were always in debt to landowners.

Women and laborers also suffered during this period. White women who had worked to end slavery were disappointed because they were not allowed to **vote** (see p. 32) immediately after the Civil War. Their lack of voting rights bothered them even more greatly when the 15th Amendment to the **U.S. Constitution**, (see Vol. 1, p. 62) was passed, granting African American men the right to vote. In the South, where many African American men were prevented from using their right to vote, there was little question that voting was out of the question for African American women as well. As industry grew, workers

1876	**1877**	**1877**	**1877**
African American artist Edward Bannister wins first prize at the Philadelphia Centennial.	**Reconstruction** ends when new president Rutherford B. Hayes withdraws federal troops from the South.	Georgia passes a law that requires voters to pay a poll tax.	African American **Exodusters** establish the town of Nicodemus in Kansas.

put in long hours for little pay. They had no insurance when they were unable to work. Children from poor families were often kept out of school to work.

The National Labor Union and the **Knights of Labor** (see p. 24) were formed in the 1860s. They tried to improve working conditions, but didn't make much progress. In 1877, the economy was very depressed and workers began to strike. President Hayes called out the army to put down a railroad strike. Laws were tightened to prevent another strike. In the 1880s, the economy improved, and the Knights of Labor, who admitted African Americans as members, gained strength. The number of strikes increased. There was another railroad strike in 1880 and a strike against the McCormick Harvester Company, a farm equipment company, which led to a riot in Chicago in 1886. A general strike in New Orleans broke out in 1891. Both steel workers in Pennsylvania and miners in Idaho struck in 1892.

RACE RELATIONS

Since colonial times, **free blacks** (see Vol.1, p. 23) had lived in all regions of the United States. Before the Civil War, they had often been denied the same rights as white Americans. After the war, amendments added to the Constitution defined citizenship and protected citizens under the law. However, these amendments did nothing to change the status of African Americans. At the end of the war, only Maine, New Hampshire, Vermont, Massachusetts and Rhode Island gave full voting rights to African American

1878	**1880**	**1881**	**1881**
Bud Fowler becomes the first African American to play on an all-white baseball team.	In *Strauder v. West Virginia* the U.S. Supreme Court rules that state laws preventing African Americans from participating in juries violates the 14th Amendment.	**Tuskegee Institute,** an all-black agricultural and vocational college, is founded in Alabama by former slave **Booker T. Washington.**	Fifty thousand **Exodusters** live in Kansas.

men. New York only let African Americans vote if they owned property. Connecticut, Wisconsin, Kansas, Ohio, Michigan and Missouri prohibited African American *suffrage*, as voting rights were called. Iowa and Minnesota, with small African American populations, allowed black men to vote. Many people did not support African American suffrage in the South.

By 1881, some 50,000 African American Exodusters (see p. 22) had moved to Kansas at the invitation of the governor. However, not all people welcomed them to Kansas.

When federal troops were removed from the south, Some white Southerners tried to keep African Americans out of government. They often called themselves "Redeemers." They thought they had come to save the South.

In 1877, Georgia required voters to pay a one dollar *poll tax*. Other Southern states soon followed. The average Southern income was just over $55 a year. One dollar was a great deal of money. South Carolina, North Carolina and Florida used ballots that were confusing for voters who could not read. Yet, more than 70 percent of eligible African Americans voted in Arkansas, Florida, North Carolina, Tennessee, and Virginia. More than 50 percent voted in Alabama, Louisiana, South Carolina and Texas.

LIMITED COOPERATION

Redeemers met with some white resistance. Some wealthy whites tried to make peace with African Americans, as long as they kept the

1882	1883	1883	1884
Lewis Latimer patents a carbon filament used in light bulbs.	Supreme Court overturns the Civil Rights Act of 1875.	Jan Ernst Matzeliger patents a machine that attaches the upper part of a shoe to the lower part.	Norbert Rillieux invents a machine that improves how sugar is processed.

upper hand. In other instances, poor and working class whites formed alliances.

In Virginia, a new political party began when Democrats used public school funds to pay off Confederate (see **Confederate States of America**, Vol. 1, p. 110) war debt. They called themselves "Readjusters," because they wanted to readjust the debt. African American and white Readjuster farmers and laborers took control of the legislature in 1879. They won the legislature and the governorship in 1881.

By the 1890s, a **Populist Party** (see p. 27) had formed among a combination of African American and white farmers and small planters. Many white political leaders realized that they had more in common with poor black farmers than with rich white planters who controlled the South. As Tom Watson, a Populist leader put it, "The accident of color can make no difference in the interest of farmers, croppers and laborers. You are kept apart that you may be separately fleeced [cheated] of your earnings." The Populists opposed lawyers, bankers and other business people who called them the New South. Lots of people thought the New South looked very much like the Old South in business dress.

Jim Crow Triumphs

When Populists began to criticize Redeemers for the way they treated African Americans, Redeemers got worried. New laws were written to make

1886–1901	1888	1890	1891
An average of 100 to 200 African Americans are lynched each year.	**W.E.B. Du Bois** graduates from Harvard University.	Mississippi's literacy law requires voters to read and interpret the **U.S. Constitution**.	Boxer George Dixon wins the U.S. Boxing Championship, becoming the first African American to hold an American sports title.

sure that African Americans were shut out once and for all. In Mississippi in 1890, voters were required to read and interpret the Constitution. White examiners tested their knowledge. Due to laws that were passed in South Carolina, most African American men lost the vote by 1895. In 1898, Louisiana said anyone who had not voted before 1867 had to take a literacy test. This allowed whites who could not read to still be able to vote. Alabama and Virginia restricted African American voting by 1902, and Georgia by 1908.

Little by little, white Democrats created what came to be called the "Solid South." African Americans were legally and socially set apart. The laws by which this was done are known as **Jim Crow Laws** (see p. 24). The name comes from a **minstrel show** (see Vol. 1, p. 86) that portrayed African Americans as simple-minded.

In 1895, 113 African Americans were lynched in the South. These illegal hangings by mobs were committed to give whites more control. **Booker T. Washington** (see p. 32), was a former enslaved person and founder of a vocational school in Tuskegee, Alabama. In a speech in 1895 he agreed to accept racial segregation in return for economic advancement. This became known as the Atlanta Compromise. Washington believed that jobs, not politics, would save the African American. His many followers hoped to end the violence. The following year, the U.S. Supreme Court ruled in *Plessy v. Ferguson* (see p. 26). The court said that Tennessee had the right to create separate facilities for African Americans on its railroads as long as they

1892	1895	1895	1896
The **Populist Party,** which includes both African American and white farmers, forms.	**Booker T. Washington,** founder of the **Tuskegee Institute,** gives his "Atlanta Compromise" speech.	**Ida B. Wells** publishes *A Red Record,* documenting lynchings.	**George Washington Carver,** an agricultural scientist, becomes a faculty member at Tuskegee Institute. In his research, he will create many new uses for peanuts, sweet potatoes and other crops.

Booker T. Washington (Library of Congress)

were equal. With the legal acceptance of "separate but equal," Jim Crow was now secure. These laws would oppress African Americans until the 1960s.

1896

National Association of Colored Women is founded.

1896

In *Plessy v. Ferguson*, the U.S. Supreme Court decides that "separate but equal" facilities for blacks and whites are legal.

A-Z of Key People, Events, and Terms

arts and literature

Minstrel shows (see Vol. 1, p. 86) were a combination of dance, folksong, and musical instruments. African American minstrel shows became more popular after the **Civil War** (see Vol. 1, p. 108). The first all–African American minstrel group was the Georgia Minstrels founded by George B. Hicks in 1865.

By 1891 African American minstrel shows became African American musical comedies. One of these, "The Creole Show," was performed at the Chicago World's Fair in 1893.

Ragtime music became popular about the same time as musical comedies. "Ragging" was practiced by many African American pianists in the 1890s. The first original ragtime song was "Tom Turpin's Harlem Rag," published in 1897. One famous ragtime tune, "Maple Leaf Rag," written by Scott Joplin in 1899, is still played today. Joplin (1868–1917) is considered the "King of Ragtime."

Scott Joplin.
(New York Public Library)

One well-known African American artist is Edward Bannister (1828–1901). Bannister studied at the Lowell Institute. His specialty was landscape art. In 1876, his painting, *Under the Oaks*, won first prize at the Philadelphia Centennial Exposition. The judges considered changing their decision when they found out that Bannister was African American (see sidebar p. 20). However, fellow artists protested and Bannister received the prize. Bannister's painting later sold for $1,500.

Another successful African American artist was Edmonia Lewis (ca.1843–1911). Lewis was the daughter of a free African American father and an Ojibwa Indian mother. She spent most of her adult life in Rome, Italy. Lewis became famous for her beautiful marble sculptures.

By 1880, photography had become an important way of preserving images. J.P. Ball (1825–1905) began his photography career before the **Civil War** (see Vol.1, p. 108). Some of his subjects were **Frederick Douglass** (see Vol.1, p. 80), Ulysses S.

In the Words of Edward M. Bannister

Edward Bannister talked about his experience with officials of the Philadelphia Centennial Exposition to fellow artist George Whitaker. These words were later repeated in Whitaker's "Reminiscences of Providence Artists."

I later learned from a newspaper ...that [entry number] "54" had received a first prize medal. I hurried to the committee room to make sure the report was true...as I jostled through [the crowd] many resented my presence, some actually commenting within my hearing, in a most **petulant** (rude) manner asking, "Why is that colored person here?" Finally I succeeded in reaching the desk where inquiries were to be made. "I want to inquire concerning 54. Is it a prize winner? "What's that to you?", he said....The looks that passed between that official and the others were unmistakable in their meaning. To them I was not an artist; simply an inquisitive colored man. Controlling myself I said with deliberation, "I am interested in the report that Under the Oaks has received a prize. I painted that picture." The explosion of a bomb could not have created more of a sensation in that room...

◀ **petulant**
rude

Source: George Whitaker, *Reminiscences of Providence Artists.*

Grant, and **Henry Highland Garnet** (see Vol. 1, p. 83). In 1887, Ball became the official photographer for several 25th anniversary celebrations of the **Emancipation Proclamation** (see Vol.1, p. 113). He also became active in the Republican Party.

African American writers such as Frederick Douglass and **W.E.B. Du Bois** (see p. 53) produced several important works of literature during the late 1800s. Anna J. Cooper wrote *A Voice from the South*, published in 1892. In this book, Cooper describes the experiences of African American women attending black colleges.

Buffalo Soldiers

After the **Civil War** (see Vol. 1, p. 108), African Americans took part in Army battles with Native Americans. Native

After the Civil War, all-black regiments served in the West, fighting in wars against Native Americans. Native Americans nicknamed them "Buffalo Soldiers" because they were so tough, and also because their hair reminded the Native Americans of buffalo. (Library of Congress)

Americans nicknamed the African Americans "Buffalo Soldiers." They chose the name for two reasons. First, the Native Americans thought the black soldiers were especially tough. Second, they had never seen tightly curled hair like that on the soldiers, and they believed it looked like buffalo hair.

The job of the Buffalo Soldiers was to protect settlers and mail routes and fight against Native American nations. In 1885, Buffalo Soldiers of the 10th Calvary were credited with capturing the feared Apache leader Geronimo.

The army placed African American soldiers in the West for many reasons. Prejudice made it difficult to station them in eastern cities. Some white believed the African American soldiers were better suited to the harsh conditions of life in the West. It also was thought that African Americans were better able than whites to survive illnesses found in the West. As a result, Buffalo Soldiers were stationed in places often rejected by white soldiers.

Buffalo Soldiers earned 14 Congressional Medals of Honor. Among those honored was Lieutenant Powhatan (*pow-HAT-tun*) Clarke. Lieutenant Clarke placed his own life at risk when he rescued a fellow soldier from Apache gunfire.

civil rights cases

In 1883, the U.S. Supreme Court heard a series of cases. These questioned whether the Civil Rights Act of 1875 was constitutional. This act said all races of people could use private facilities such as theaters, railroad cars, and hotels. In 1883 the Supreme Court said the Civil Rights Act of 1875 was unconstitutional. It said that the federal government did not have authority to regulate the private conduct of individuals in regard to race.

In a dissenting opinion, Justice John Harlan argued that the government had to protect individuals against discrimination. He based his opinion on the 13th and 14th Amendments, which ended slavery and gave African Americans the same rights as all citizens.

education

After the **Civil War** (see Vol.1, p. 108), segregation laws kept African Americans out of many schools. In spite of this some were very successful in education. In 1876 Yale University awarded the first doctorate degree in physics to Edward Bouchet, an African American. In 1896 Harvard awarded a doctorate in history to **W.E.B. Du Bois** (see p. 53). Some colleges were established to admit African Americans.

By 1900, 2,000 African Americans held college degrees. Over 21,000 were schoolteachers. Yet, at the turn of the century, 45 percent of African Americans could not read. Most schools for African American children were very poor.

election of 1876

In 1876 the Republican, Rutherford B. Hayes ran against the Democrat, Samuel J. Tilden. The election was very close and some states sent in conflicting results. There was so much confusion, the winner had to be decided by Congress.

A Senate committee gave the election to Hayes. In return Hayes ended **Reconstruction** (see Vol.1, p. 123) soon after taking office.

Exodusters (*ECK-so-dust-ers*)

During the late 1870s and early 1880s, thousands of African Americans fled the Deep South and moved west of the Mississippi River. Two leaders of this *exodus* were Henry Adams, from Louisiana, and Benjamin "Pap" Singleton, from Tennessee. Singleton was an ex-slave who called himself "Moses," and his followers "Exodusters." This was because he thought they were like the story of Moses who led the exodus of the Jews out of Egypt.

The Election of 1876

Although Democrat Samuel Tilden won more popular votes than his Republican opponent, Rutherford B. Hayes, the election of 1876 was decided in the U.S. Congress. Hayes was awarded more electoral votes when he agreed to withdraw federal troops from the South. His bargain ended Reconstruction, and the enforcement of many of the civil rights protections that African Americans had gained after the Civil War.

Candidate	Party	Popular Votes	Electoral Votes
Rutherford B. Hayes	Republican	4,033,768	185
Samuel Tilden	Democrat	4,285,922	184

In 1877 Adams and Singleton convinced over 20,000 African Americans to travel to the Kansas prairie. The South was against this movement. An armed group of southern whites threatened to close the Mississippi River by blockading river landings. They also threatened to sink all boats carrying African Americans.

One famous Exoduster was Edwin P. McCabe. McCabe told African Americans to move to the Oklahoma Territory. He had a

This African American family was one of many that settled on the Great Plains in the late 1800s. (Library of Congress)

vision of the territory becoming a black state with himself as governor. McCabe helped to start several all black towns in Oklahoma. However, when Oklahoma became a state in 1907, it passed several **Jim Crow Laws** (see below). These laws made life difficult for African Americans.

Jim Crow Laws

After **Reconstruction** (see Vol. 1, p. 123), blacks and whites often traveled in the same railroad cars, used the same public facilities, and ate in the same restaurants. Soon competition for city jobs increased between African Americans and whites. White-controlled city governments passed laws that limited the freedom of African Americans. These were called Jim Crow laws, named after a minstrel show character. Jim Crow laws allowed segregation within all areas of society. They supported the idea of "separate but equal" being the only acceptable way of life. The U.S. Supreme Court supported Jim Crow laws when it said the Civil Rights Act of 1875 was unconstitutional (see **civil rights cases**, p. 21).

States continued to pass Jim Crow laws for many years. The idea of "separate but equal" was part of American life well into the 20th century. Private and public facilities, such as washrooms, drinking fountains, restaurants, schools, hospital services and transportation were separated by race. The quality of public facilities for African Americans was not really equal. It was far below the quality of facilities for whites.

In 1954, in the case *Brown v. Board of Education* (see p. 81), the U.S. Supreme Court decided that separate but equal public education was unconstitutional. With that decision, all laws allowing public facilities to be separate but equal were questioned.

Knights of Labor

The Knights of Labor, the first union to admit African Americans as members, was a labor union formed in 1869. Originally, all-white, by 1886 it had 700,000 members including African American laborers, shopkeepers, and farmers. The group supported an 8-hour workday at a time when 10-hour workdays were common. It also asked for child labor laws. The union did not favor strikes to settle disputes between labor and management. However, there were violent labor strikes. These hurt the reputation of the

Jim Crow Laws

These are examples of some of the Jim Crow laws passed in various states during the late 1800s. Other states passed laws similar to the ones listed here.

Buses: All passenger stations in this state operated by any motor transportation company shall have separate waiting rooms or space and separate ticket windows for white and colored races. (Alabama)

Burial: The officer in charge shall not bury, or allow to be buried, any colored persons upon ground set apart or used for the burial of white persons. (Georgia)

The Blind: The board of trustees shall maintain a separate building on separate ground for the admission, care, instruction, and support of all blind persons of the colored or black race. (Louisiana)

Education: Separate schools shall be maintained for the children of the white and colored races. (Mississippi)

Intermarriage: All marriages between a white person and a Negro person or between a white person and a person of Negro descent to the fourth generation inclusive, are hereby forever prohibited. (Florida)

Lunch Counters: No persons, firms, or corporations, who or which furnish meals to passengers at station restaurants or station eating houses, in times limited by common carriers of said passengers, shall furnish said meals to white and colored passengers in the same room, or at the same table, or at the same counter. (South Carolina)

Railroads: The conductors or managers on all such railroads shall have power, and are hereby required, to assign to each white or colored passenger his or her respective car, coach, or compartment. If the passenger fails to disclose his race, the conductor and managers, acting in good faith shall be the sole judges of his race. (Virginia)

Textbooks: Books shall not be interchangeable between the white and colored schools, but shall be continued to be used by the race first using them. (North Carolina)

Knights of Labor. By 1886 many people who had belonged to the Knights of Labor joined the American Federation of Labor instead.

lynching

Lynching is putting someone accused of a crime to death by hanging without holding a fair trial. The term comes from Charles Lynch, a Virginia planter in the 1700s. Lynching became common following **Reconstruction** (see Vol. 1, p. 123).

Lynchings occurred most often in the South. White mobs terrorized African Americans. They controlled communities through fear. African Americans could be lynched for murder, insulting a white person, or applying for a job that a white man also wanted.

Lynchings often went unpunished. Sometimes law officers even took part in the lynchings. Official records show that between 1882 and 1968, 4,743 men and women were lynched. Of these, 3,446 were African Americans. Between 1882 and 1901 whites lynched 100 to 200 African Americans every year. The year most lynchings occurred was in 1882 when an average of 4 African Americans were lynched every week. In truth, the actual number of African Americans lynched will never be known.

National Association of Colored Women

The National Association of Colored Women was founded in 1896 in Washington, D.C. This group educated poor people on health care concerns. It also began a nurses' training school in New Orleans for African American women.

Members of this group wrote petitions for the repeal of **Jim Crow Laws** (see p. 24) and an end to segregation. Within five years, the group had grown from one chapter to chapters in 26 states.

Plessy v. Ferguson

In 1890, Louisiana passed the "Act to Promote the Comfort of Passengers." This law legalized the practice of segregating African Americans from white railroad passengers by forcing African Americans to sit in separate railroad cars.

In 1890 Homer Plessy, a black man, was arrested for riding in an all-white railroad car. In 1892 Plessy challenged the 1890 Louisiana law in court. He said that he had refused to ride in the "colored" section of the train. He sued the railroad, basing his lawsuit on the 13th and 14th Amendments (see **U.S. Constitution**, Vol. 1, p. 62).

The railroads secretly supported Plessy because it was costly to have separate cars for the races. However, Plessy lost in Louisiana state court. The case was appealed all the way to the Supreme Court and became the 1896 landmark case titled *Plessy* v. *Ferguson*.

The U.S. Supreme Court upheld the practice of "separate but equal." The Court ruled that the Louisiana law did not violate

Plessy v. Ferguson (1896)

In this landmark case the U.S. Supreme Court ruled 7-1 that the doctrine of "separate but equal" did not go against the U.S. Constitution.

Justice Brown wrote the majority opinion.
"...we think the enforced separation of the races, as applied to the internal commerce of the state, neither abridges the privileges or immunities of the colored man, deprives him of his property without due process of law, nor denies him the equal protection of the laws, within the meaning of the 14th Amendment."

In a dissenting opinion, Justice Harlan wrote:
"...in view of the constitution, in the eye of the law, there is in this country no superior, dominant, ruling class of citizens. There is no caste here. Our constitution is color-blind, and neither knows nor tolerates classes among citizens. In respect of civil rights, all citizens are equal before the law."

Source: National Archives

◀ **abridges**
to make less or take away something

◀ **immunities**
freedom or protection

◀ **caste**
division of people by social class

the 14th Amendment. Justice John Marshall Harlan was the only dissenter. He stated that the U.S. Constitution was "color-blind." He said that the decision would open the door to equally unfair laws and social practices.

Populist Party

The Populist Party, also called the People's Party, was formed in 1892 as a reaction to the power of big business over farmers. During the late 1800s farmers in the West and in the South had large troubles. There was a drought in the West and low cotton prices in the South. This caused farmers to have to borrow much money. Big businesses such as banks and railroads held much power over the farmers.

In 1878 African Americans became active in the Populist movement. About 1.25 million out of a U.S. population of about 5 million African Americans joined the newly formed Colored

Farmer's Alliance. This group, along with the all-white Farmers Alliance and the Knights of Labor, became the strength behind the Populist Party. The Party's 1896 presidential campaign called for an end to corporate wrongs. It asked for assistance for poor farmers and city workers. Populists in western states demanded the right to vote for women nationwide.

Disagreements within the Populist Party caused it to fail. Many of its ideas continued into the next century.

Science and Technology

African Americans helped advance technology both before and after the **Civil War** (see Vol. 1, p. 108). Patent rules in 1793 and in 1836 allowed enslaved Africans to patent their inventions. However, masters claimed ownership of many inventions designed by enslaved Africans. Some think that pre–Civil War inventions such as the cotton gin and the grain harvester were really invented by African Americans.

With the passage of the 13th and 14th Amendments (see **U.S. Constitution**, Vol. 1, p. 62), African Americans were free to patent their inventions. African Americans filed many patents during the late 1800s.

In the years following the Civil War, African Americans invented machines that made farming easier. Charles T. Christmas was a former Mississippi enslaved person. In 1880 he patented a device that simplified the baling of cotton. In 1884 Lockrum Blue, also African American, patented a machine to remove the hard shell from corn.

Other inventions helped the railroad and other businesses. H.H. Reynolds was a porter working for the Pullman Company. Reynolds invented a ventilator that allowed air to flow into cars, but also kept out the dust. The Pullman Company tried to say they invented the device. Reynolds sued the Pullman Company and won.

Another inventor, Jan Ernst Matzeliger patented the "shoe lasting" machine in

Jan Matzeliger (Library of Congress)

1883. The last is the upper part of the shoe. The shoe lasting machine made the attachment of the last to the bottom sole simpler. Matzeliger's machine cut the cost of shoe production and made it faster.

In 1884 Granville T. Woods received a patent for a telephone transmitter. He later sold the patent to Alexander Graham Bell. Woods patented over 50 inventions. These included air brakes, a train warning system, and an egg-hatching machine.

Science took another leap forward in 1882 with Lewis Latimer's patent of the carbon filament used in the light bulb. Latimer also made drawings for Alexander Graham Bell's telephone. He also worked with inventor Thomas Edison.

Granville T. Woods (Library of Congress)

One of the greatest African American scientists of all time was **George Washington Carver** (see p. 51). Carver researched uses for peanuts, sweet potatoes, soybeans and other crops. Carver discovered over 300 uses for peanuts including face powder, a milk substitute, and printer ink. His study of sweet potatoes identified 118 uses including rubber production.

sharecropping

In sharecropping, individuals trade labor and a share of the crops in exchange for animals, lodging, land, tools, and seed from a land owner. Sharecropping was seen as a way for former enslaved African Americans to become independent.

In practice, sharecropping became a way for landowners to enslave poor farmers. Charges for board, lodging, washing, and store items amounted to more than the pay for work and harvest. Tenants were not allowed to leave the land until the debt was paid. With the debt increasing every month many African American sharecroppers were once again forced to work for white landlords.

sports

Before the **Civil War** (see Vol. 1, p. 108) enslaved African Americans were not allowed to take part in professional sports. This changed during the post–Civil War years. The first African American to hold an American sports title was George Dixon. He was only 5'3" tall, and weighed 100 pounds. He won an international boxing championship on June 17, 1890. Soon after, on March 31, 1891, Dixon won the American title against Cal McCarthy.

On September 6, 1892, Dixon beat Jack Skelly in a fight that took place in New Orleans. From then on, southern white boxers refused to fight black fighters.

There was also discrimination in baseball. In 1871 the National Association of Professional Baseball Players barred African Americans from membership. However, African American players continued to play on several all-black teams. Race barriers in baseball were broken when, in 1878, Bud Fowler became the first African American to join an all-white professional team. In 1883 Moses Walker became the second African American to play professional baseball. Before playing in the major league, Walker played baseball for Oberlin College where he studied. He also attended the University of Michigan law school.

In 1887 the manager of the Chicago White Stockings refused to allow his team to play against Newark unless Moses Walker and another African American, George Stovey, left the field. Later that year white members of the St. Louis Browns refused to play the all-black New York Cuban Giants. Until 1947 Moses Walker and his brother, Welday, were the only two African American baseball players to play in the major leagues.

Strauder v. West Virginia

In *Strauder* v. *West Virginia*, the Supreme Court ruled in 1880 that state laws preventing African Americans from being on juries violated the 14th Amendment. Strauder, an African American, had been convicted of murder by an all-white jury. West Virginia, like many other states at the time, did not allow African Americans on juries. Strauder appealed his murder conviction to the U.S. Supreme Court. He said that not having a jury of his peers violated his right to a fair trial. The U.S. Supreme Court agreed.

Strauder v. West Virginia

The Supreme Court's *Strauder v. West Virginia* decision, in which the court decided that an all-white jury in West Virginia had denied the defendant a fair trial, was a rare victory for African Americans. Below, Justice Strong gives his reason for the court's decision:

"...it is hard to see why the statute of West Virginia should not be regarded as discriminating against a colored man when he is put upon trial for an alleged criminal offense against the State...Is not protection of life and liberty against race or color prejudice, a right, a legal right, under the [14th] constitutional amendment? And how can it be maintained that compelling a colored man to submit to a trial for his life by a jury drawn from a panel from which the State has expressly excluded every man of his race, because of color alone, ...is not a denial to him of equal legal protection?...We do not believe the 14th Amendment was ever intended to prohibit this...its design was to protect an emancipated race, and to strike down all possible legal discriminations against those who belong to it."

Source: National Archives

Terrell, Mary Church

Mary Church Terrell (1863 –1954) was one of the first African American women to receive a college degree from Oberlin College in Ohio. In 1895 she founded the National Association of Colored Women. She became the first woman to serve on the District of Columbia Board of Education. In 1940 Terrell wrote *A Colored Woman in a White World*. In this book she described how racism affected her life. Terrell spent her life advocating for equality for African American women in white society.

Mary Church Terrell.
(Library of Congress)

Tuskegee Institute

The Tuskegee Institute began as the Tuskegee Normal and Industrial Institute in Tuskegee, Alabama in 1881. The mission of the Tuskegee Institute was to train African Americans to be schoolteachers and skilled trades people.

Booker T. Washington (see p. 32) was Tuskegee's founder and first administrator. The AME Zion Church (see **African Methodist Episcopal Church**, Vol. 1, p. 46) allowed Tuskegee to use its church and a small shack nearby. While classes were being held at the church, plans to build the school took shape. A farm was purchased and money was raised. Booker T. Washington, along with his staff and a small group of students, built the first school buildings. In 1885 the Tuskegee Institute graduated its first class. The school continues to operate to this day, as Tuskegee University.

voting

The 15th Amendment to the **U.S. Constitution** (see Vol. 1, p. 62) was passed in 1870. This amendment granted voting rights to African Americans. Still, many states tried to prevent African Americans from voting. They passed laws that made voting difficult. One such law, called the *grandfather clause*, said an African American man could only vote if his father or grandfather could have voted in 1867. Other laws said in order to vote a man had to be able to read and write. Some laws asked an individual to follow a complicated set of written instructions before he was allowed to vote. *Poll taxes* required men to pay a sum of money before they were allowed to vote. All these laws resulted in reducing the number of African Americans who could vote. They also prevented some poor white men from voting.

Washington, Booker T.

Booker T. Washington was born into slavery in 1856. His enslaved mother was a cook on a Virginia plantation. His father was white, though little is known about him.

Following emancipation, Washington moved with his mother and stepfather to West Virginia. He worked in the coal mines and attended school when possible. He returned to Virginia in 1871 to enroll in the all–African American Hampton Institute. He later became a faculty member. Washington left the Hampton Institute in 1881 to found the Tuskegee Normal and Industrial Institute. This later became the **Tuskegee Institute** (see p. 31).

When the Tuskegee Institute first opened it had a faculty of three. Together they taught 37 students. When Washington died in 1915, the Tuskegee Institute had grown to a faculty of 180 and 1,500 students. Much of the school's success was due to Washington's ability to raise funds from the white community to build and to support the school.

Washington was criticized for his belief that African Americans should concentrate their education on vocational

Booker T. Washington became the first African American to be invited to the White House when he visited with Theodore Roosevelt. In the picture above, Washington (center) is seen with President William Howard Taft (left), who followed Roosevelt, and businessman, Andrew Carnegie (right). (Library of Congress)

needs, not on a university curriculum. He was also criticized for not taking part in the 1909 founding of the National Association for the Advancement of Colored People (NAACP). Washington received his strongest criticism for what seemed to be an acceptance of segregation.

In 1885 Washington spoke at the Cotton States and International Exposition. He made a speech later known as the Atlanta Compromise. In his speech, Washington talked of peace, prosperity, and the continuation of segregation. He said, "In all things that are purely social we can be as separate as the fingers, yet one as the hand in all things essential to mutual progress."

Wells, Ida B.

Ida Wells (1862–1931) was one of the founders of the **National Association for the Advancement of Colored People (NAACP)** (see p. 62) in 1909. She spent her life fighting against white oppression of African Americans. In 1884 she sued the Cleveland and Ohio Railroad after she was forced to leave the first-class section. She won the case, but the Tennessee Supreme Court later reversed the decision.

Wells openly challenged the lynching of African Americans. In an article in the *Memphis Free Speech and Headlight* on March 9, 1892, Wells protested the lynching of three African Americans who had tried to defend their property against whites. Wells argued that many of the crimes whites accused African Americans of in order to justify lynchings were unfounded. After this, Wells was banned from living or working in Memphis, Tennessee.

The Red Record

In this excerpt from *The Red Record* Ida B. Wells describes the injustice and lawlessness of lynching:

In lynching, opportunity is not given the Negro to defend himself against the unsupported accusations of white men and women. The word of the accuser is held to be true and the excited blood-thirsty mob demands that the rule of law be reversed and instead of proving the accused to be guilty, the victim of their hate and revenge must prove himself innocent. No evidence he can offer will satisfy the mob; he is bound hand and foot and swung into eternity. Then to excuse its infamy, the mob almost invariably reports the monstrous falsehood that its victim made a full confession before he was hanged.

Source: Ida Wells, *The Red Record*

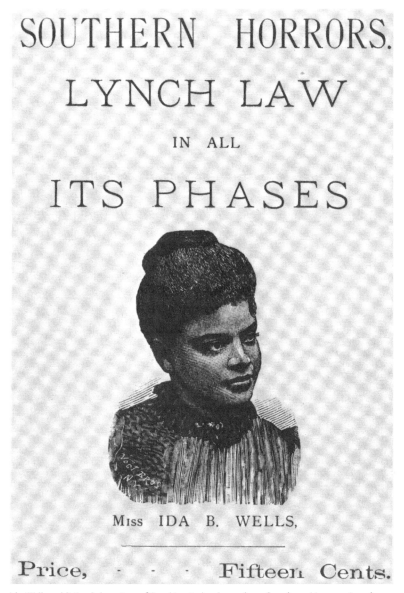

SOUTHERN HORRORS.

LYNCH LAW

IN ALL

ITS PHASES

MISS IDA B. WELLS,

Price, · · · Fifteen Cents.

Ida Wells publicized the crime of lynching in books such as *Southern Horrors: Lynch Law in All Its Phases*. (New York Public Library)

Wells continued to speak out and write about the practice of lynching. In 1892 she wrote *Southern Horrors: Lynch Law in All Its Phases*. This gave details of lynchings in the South. In 1895 Ida B. Wells finished her work on a pamphlet called *The Red Record*. In it she kept track of the number of lynchings that took place in the United States from 1892 to 1894. She explained that many white Southerners said lynching was just punishment for African American assaults against white women. Wells showed that only one-third of all African American lynchings were for assaults against white women.

Wells asked that communities be punished for allowing lynching. She also asked that whites and African Americans be treated the same in criminal matters. She wanted laws passed to ensure that African Americans would be protected under the 14th Amendment. She felt that lynching would only end through public pressure and fairness in the courts.

Lift Every Voice
The Early 20th Century, 1897-1945

"We refuse to allow the impression to remain that the Negro-American assents to inferiority, is submissive under oppression and apologetic before insults. Through helplessness we may submit, but the voice of protest of ten million Americans must never cease to assail the ears of their fellows so long as America is unjust."

—The Niagara Movement, 1905

Throughout the first half of the 20th century, African Americans continued to hope for justice and equality. They tried many ways to gain power and acceptance. None of these was completely successful.

African Americans were denied true freedom by **Jim Crow Laws** (see p. 24) in the South and "unofficial" segregation in the North. There were also other factors. One was the immigration of large numbers of people from Central and Southern Europe.

NEW PEOPLE, NEW PROBLEMS
The immigrants who began to arrive in the 1890s were different from those of previous generations. From the start, the United States has been a nation of immigrants. Most immigrants came from Western Europe and were Protestant. This new wave of immigrants came from eastern and southern Europe and Asia. Most were Roman Catholic and Jewish. By 1914, 15 million newcomers had arrived, mostly in northern cities. Factories and mines welcomed them, but often their neighbors did not. By 1915, the **Ku Klux Klan** (see Vol. 1, p. 118) had been revived.

Lynching (see p. 25) went unchecked. Between 1900 and 1915, white mobs lynched 1,446 African Americans and 205 whites. Usually the victims were black men who either tried to vote, testified in court against a white person, or in some way seemed disrespectful. Black women and whites who sided with African American men were also lynched. After being beaten and abused the victim was hung in a public place. Repeated protests by African Americans were ignored. To the Klan and those who gave it silent support, true Americans could be only white and Protestant.

SOUTHERN MISERY FUELS MIGRATION

Nine out of 10 African Americans lived in the South in 1900. Only 8,000 out of 970,000 black young people there attended high school. Black colleges and vocational schools like **Tuskegee Institute** (see p. 31) served some students, but there were not enough of these schools. Young African American people and their families had no legal protections. Their parents could not vote. However, most whites supported **Booker T. Washington**'s (see p. 32) position that African Americans should work hard and not challenge segregation.

African Americans sought comfort from the church and from music. A number of great African American musicians were born between the end of the **Civil War** (see Vol. 1, p. 108) and 1900. They included ragtime piano composer Scott Joplin; W.C. Handy, whose "Memphis Blues" was the first blues com-

Timeline

1900–1915 ◎ 1903

Between 1900 and 1915, white mobs **lynch** 1,446 African Americans.

W. E. B. Du Bois publishes his best-known book, *The Souls of Black Folks*.

position; Dixieland **jazz** (see p. 58) greats **Louis Armstrong** (see p. 47) and Jelly Roll Morton; blues singer Bessie Smith, and jazz bandleader and composer Duke Ellington. They began a musical culture that would influence the entire nation.

A smaller number of African Americans supported **W. E. B. Du Bois** (see p. 53). Du Bois was a professor in Atlanta. He had been the first African American to earn a doctorate from Harvard. Although he respected Booker T. Washington, he disagreed with him. "The way for a people to attain their reasonable rights is not by voluntarily throwing them away," he said. Because he was born in the North, Du Bois was not close to sharecroppers and field hands. He wanted to train the most intelligent African Americans to lead the way. He called these the "Talented Tenth." Beginning in 1905, Du Bois led a group seeking full equality for African Americans. Meeting in Canada, they called themselves the **Niagara Movement** (see p. 63). In 1910, they joined a group of liberal whites in forming a new organization. They called it the **National Association for the Advancement of Colored People**, or **NAACP** (see p. 62). Du Bois was made editor of the organization's newspaper, the *Crisis*.

By this time, many more African Americans were fed up with southern life. They moved to New York, Chicago, Detroit, Buffalo and other Northern cities. This movement was often called the **Great Migration** (see p. 57). It began when the United States was preparing for **World War I** (see p. 67). This caused factory jobs to open up. In the North, segregation was a matter of custom, not law.

1905	**1905**	**1906**	**1909**
The **Niagara Movement**, an African American civil rights organization, is founded.	The *Chicago Defender*, an important newspaper serving Chicago's African American community, begins publication.	In the **Brownsville Affair**, a group of African American soldiers are falsely convicted of killing a white man and shooting a policeman.	The **National Association for the Advancement of Colored People (NAACP)** is founded.

World War I started in Europe in 1914, but the United States did not join until 1917. The war ended in 1918. Only 42,000 of the 380,000 African Americans who served were allowed to take part in combat. The rest worked as laborers in support of the war effort. White commanders said African Americans would not perform well in battle. However, African American troops that were allowed to fight did perform very well. About 750 of them died and 10 times more were injured. The U.S. and France awarded combat medals to 550 African American soldiers. African Americans who fought abroad discovered that French society was less prejudiced. This made some men very angry, but others gained hope that U.S. society could one day improve.

For some African Americans, the only solution seemed to be to return to Africa. African Americans had been joining with others around the world to promote unity and celebrate African culture. A series of conferences began in 1900 in London, England. Other conferences were held at Tuskegee, Alabama and in Paris, France; Lisbon, Portugal; and Brussels, Belgium. Some people began to support formation of a new black nation with black leaders. **Marcus Garvey** (see p. 56), a Jamaican, believed that people of African ancestry should set themselves apart from a corrupt white society. He founded the Universal Negro Improvement Association in Kingston, Jamaica, in 1914. He moved it to New York in 1916. Garvey started a shipping line called the Black Star to take people to Africa. He attracted half a million followers. Although his

1912	1914–1918	1917	1917
Composer W. C. Handy writes "The Memphis Blues," which becomes known as the first blues song ever written.	**World War I** is fought in Europe.	The United States enters **World War I**.	In what becomes known as the **Houston Mutiny**, 17 African American soldiers riot against **Jim Crow Laws**.

organization elected him President of Africa, Garvey never made it there. The Black Star line went broke and he was arrested on charges of mail fraud and *deported.*

PROGRESS AND RETREAT

The years between 1895 and 1920 are often called the Progressive Era. During that time, organized labor gained strength in the workplace. The government broke up some *trusts* that kept business and wealth in the hands of only a few. Many laws were passed to protect labor's safety and improve public health. The U.S. Constitution was also amended to allow for a federal income tax, the direct election of senators, the right of women to vote, and the prohibition of alcohol.

Yet African Americans did not make much progress. Labor unions often excluded blacks. The election of Woodrow Wilson to the Presidency in 1912 and again in 1916 was a setback for African Americans. Wilson segregated government offices in Washington. Booker T. Washington said that he had rarely seen black morale so low. In 1917, the NAACP organized a march of 15,000 African Americans down New York's Fifth Avenue. They marched in silence to protest America's silence in the face of the horrible treatment of African Americans.

THE HARLEM RENAISSANCE

By 1922, the United States produced one-third of the world's industrial out-

1919	**1921**	**1928**	**1931**
During the summer of 1919, race-related riots take place in 26 cities, as white soldiers return from war to find their former jobs taken by African Americans. The bloody fights earn the summer the nickname **Red Summer**.	The **Tulsa Riot**, one of the worst racial disturbances of the 20th century, takes place. The Greenwood District of Tulsa, a mostly black neighborhood, is destroyed.	*Amos 'n' Andy*, a controversial radio show that stars two white actors playing African Americans, begins its 32 years on radio.	In the *Scottsboro Boys* case, nine African Americans are arrested and convicted of assault on two white women, despite charges of an unfair trial.

put. For most Americans, this meant a bigger paycheck and a higher standard of living. Some of it benefited African Americans. New York City's Harlem was one of the chief destinations of the Great Migration. Soon it would have more African Americans than Birmingham, Memphis, and St. Louis put together. It became a magnet for artists, writers, musicians, theater people, and political leaders (see **arts and literature**, p. 45, and **Harlem Renaissance**, p. 58). Besides homes, there were fashionable clubs and ballrooms, and churches. There were also businesses, *settlement houses* and civil rights organizations. Even white people liked the new jazz from musicians like Duke Ellington and **Louis Armstrong** (see p. 47) and singer Ella Fitzgerald. They liked to dance the Lindy and the Charleston. African Americans invented these dances. For the first time in American history, being African American was fashionable.

No one could have been happier about this than James Weldon Johnson. He was the executive secretary of the NAACP. Johnson had been a diplomat and was also a poet and composer. He and his brother, John Rosamund, had come from Florida to New York to produce musicals. Together they wrote "Lift Ev'ry Voice and Sing." This was sometimes called the Negro national anthem.

Now Johnson had company. He encouraged poets such as Langston Hughes and Countee Cullen. Writer Zora Neale Hurston shared his interest in black *folklore*. One of the most famous places to hear that music—the **Cotton Club** (see p. 52)—featured many of the era's great performers. Everywhere there was music — gospel, blues and jazz. This new culture came

1931

The **Nation of Islam** is founded in Detroit. The group, which shares many of the same principles as the religion of Islam, will grow to great influence in the coming years.

1933

President Franklin Roosevelt begins **New Deal** programs to help put Americans back to work during the Great Depression.

1933

Nathan Ross Margold, a lawyer for the NAACP, publishes a paper outlining a strategy for countering the "separate but equal" doctrine. The paper will eventually help overturn legalized segregation.

1937

The Negro American League, an all-African American baseball league, is founded, becoming the latest in a series of **negro league** baseball organizations.

to be called the "Harlem Renaissance."

During the 1920s and early 1930s, Harlem was the place to be. When the stock market crashed in 1929, the boom that had been called "the Roaring Twenties" was over. As the Great Depression grew, wealthy white patrons who had made Harlem their playground stayed at home.

THE NEW DEAL AND WORLD WAR II

After the stock market crashed, white unemployment rose 20 percent. African American unemployment rose 50 percent. Many went hungry or became homeless. Republican President Herbert Hoover tried to stop the slide. He was not successful. Democrat Franklin D. Roosevelt was elected President. He promised "a new deal for the American people."

Roosevelt's New Deal put millions back to work on government projects. It also gave financial aid to the needy. Roosevelt protected certain parts of the economy, including labor unions. Roosevelt wife, Eleanor, was a powerful advocate for African Americans. She arranged the appointment of educator **Mary McLeod Bethune** (see p. 48) to head the National Youth Administration. They became friends. The President formed an unofficial **Black Cabinet** (see p. 49) to advise him. The African American community had never before received such attention. For the first time, many African Americans who could vote, switched to the Democratic Party.

Ten years after the market crash, **World War II** (see p. 67) broke out in

1937	**1939**	**1939–1945**	**1941**
Adam Clayton Powell, Jr. becomes pastor of the **Abyssinian Baptist Church** in New York's Harlem. In 1945 Powell will become New York's first African American congressman.	**Charles Drew**, an African American, opens the first blood bank in the U.S.	World War II is fought. After the United States joins the war in 1941, segregated African American units are formed.	President Roosevelt ends segregation in defense plants. The order comes due to pressure from A. Philip Randolph, who had threatened to send 100,000 African Americans to Washington to protest.

Europe. Once again, Germany (this time with Italy) fought against Britain and France. And once again, the United States did not join in right away. But when Germany's ally Japan attacked the American fleet at Pearl Harbor in December 1941, the United States declared war.

FDR banned racial discrimination in defense industries. This was in response to a threat from A. Phillip Randolph of the **Brotherhood of Sleeping Car Porters** (see p. 50). He said that civil rights leaders would form a **March on Washington** (see p. 60). However, the armed services, except for the merchant marines, remained strictly segregated. More than a million African American men and women were enlisted. Approximately half served overseas and 5,000 became officers. Although African Americans fought bravely, not one received one of the 433 Medals of Honor awarded during the war. In 1997, after a review of the records, seven black soldiers were finally awarded medals. Only one, Vernon Baker, was still alive.

Returning to a segregated society after the war was particularly difficult for African Americans. At the NAACP, the Urban League and the Congress for Racial Equality, plans were underway to end segregation once and for all. President Harry Truman, who took office when Roosevelt died in 1945, was a staunch ally. Hope was still alive.

1945 ◦ ◦ 1945 ◦ ◦ 1945 ◦ ◦ 1945

Japan bombs the American naval base at Pearl Harbor, Hawaii, entering the U.S. into **World War II**. During battle, an African American cook named Dorie Miller, drags the ship's wounded captain to safety, and then takes control of a machine gun to defend his ship.

African American officers protest the segregation of officers clubs in the **Freeman Field Mutiny**.

President Franklin D. Roosevelt dies in office. Harry Truman becomes President.

Atomic bombs are dropped on Japan. **World War II** ends.

A-Z of Key People, Events, and Terms

Abyssinian Baptist Church

The Abyssinian (*ab-uh-SIN-nee-in*) Baptist Church was established in 1808 by a group of wealthy traders from Abyssinia (today Ethiopia). The Abyssinian Baptist Church became the first African American Baptist church in New York. It also was the first non-segregated Baptist church. In 1937 Adam Clayton Powell, Jr. succeeded his father as pastor of the church. In 1945 Powell became New York's first African American congressman.

Amos 'n' Andy

Amos 'n' Andy began as a radio show on March 19, 1928. The show was the work of Freeman Gosden ("Amos") and Charles Correll ("Andy"). They were two white actors who had been directors of black minstrel shows. The show portrayed the lives of two urban African Americans. One of them, Amos, was a quiet family man, while the other, Andy, was a foolish bumbler. By 1930 the show had over 40 million listeners. It became the longest running radio show in radio history. *Amos 'n' Andy* also aired as a television show between 1951 and 1953. Although the show had the first all-black cast on television, the African American community criticized the show. They did not like the way it portrayed blacks. The radio show stayed on the air until 1960.

arts and literature

Beginning in the late 1890s, jazz became a very popular form of music. Such great jazz musicians as **Louis Armstrong** (see p. 47), Fletcher Henderson, and James P. Johnson helped create the great jazz sound of the times (see **jazz**, p. 58).

Swing music was very popular during the 1930s and early 1940s. Two great African American swing musicians were Edward "Duke" Ellington and **Count Basie** (see p. 48). In 1957 Basie became the first American bandleader to perform before the Queen of England.

Roland Hayes (Library of Congress)

Paul Robeson (Library of Congress)

There were also several excellent African American opera singers. One was Roland Hayes. He first sang in New York in 1923. His mother had been enslaved. Another was Lillian Evanti. In 1934 she sang for President and Mrs. Roosevelt at the White House.

Perhaps the greatest opera singer of her time was Marian Anderson. In 1939 the Daughters of the American Revolution (DAR) would not allow Anderson to sing at Constitution Hall in Washington, D.C. This was because she was an African American. In protest, Eleanor Roosevelt resigned from the DAR. She invited Anderson to sing at the Lincoln Memorial on Easter. Over 75,000 people were there. In 1955 Anderson was invited to sing with New York's Metropolitan Opera Company.

"Clorindy or The Origin of the Cakewalk" was a musical written by Paul Laurence Dunbar and William Marion Cook. It opened on Broadway on July 5, 1898. It had a cast of 26 African Americans. It featured the cakewalk, a popular dance that had its roots in the days of enslavement of African Americans. In 1921 "Shuffle Along" became the first musical revue written, produced, and performed by African Americans on a New York Broadway stage. Eubie Blake and Noble Sissle were African Americans who wrote music and lyrics. One of their musical revues featured a dance called the Charleston. This became the most popular dance of the 1920s.

One of the most successful African American singer/actors of the time was

Paul Robeson. He attended both Rutgers University and the Columbia University School of Law. He appeared in many roles throughout the 1920s, 1930s, and 1940s.

Aaron Douglas and Archibald Motley were African American artists. Motley's work portrayed life in African American communities. Richmond Barthe was a painter who became a sculptor. Other famous African American sculptors were Sargent Johnson and Augusta Savage.

The **Harlem Renaissance** (see p. 58) produced many talented writers. **W.E.B. Du Bois** (see p. 53), James Weldon Johnson, Jessie Fauset, Alain Locke, Walter White and Charles Johnson helped African Americans advance in theater, literature and civil rights. In 1925 Alain Locke put together a book titled *The New Negro*. This was a collection of poetry, prose and artwork of artists from Harlem. It brought international fame to the Harlem Renaissance.

Sculptor Augusta Savage (Library of Congress)

Langston Hughes was a prolific and talented writer. He wrote over 30 plays, two novels, three volumes of short stories, children's books and over 17 books of poetry. His first book of poems, *The Weary Blues* (1926), is filled with the expressions of African American life in America.

Armstrong, Louis

Louis Armstrong (1901 – 1971) was one of the most influential jazz musicians of all time. He was born poor in New Orleans and grew up in a home for boys. He was befriended by the great jazz cornet player, Joe (King) Oliver. He bought Armstrong his first cornet and gave him lessons. By the age of 18 Armstrong was playing with Kid Ory's band in New Orleans. He joined King Oliver's Creole Band in 1922. Soon after, Armstrong gave up the cornet for the trumpet.

A young Louis Armstrong is seen here, third from right, with King Oliver's band. (Library of Congress).

For many years Armstrong was the featured player in big bands. He played for famous African American singers Ella Fitzgerald and Bessie Smith. He also appeared in over 50 movies and made over 1,500 recordings. He entertained until his death in 1971.

Basie, William "Count"

Count Basie (1904–1984) was born in Red Bank, New Jersey. He began playing piano at the age of six. He organized his own jazz band and began touring the United States in the 1930s. The popularity of Basie's big band swing style music continued for several decades and influenced a whole generation of musicians of all races.

Bethune, Mary McLeod

Mary McLeod Bethune. (Library of Congress)

Mary McLeod was born on a rice and cotton farm in South Carolina in 1875. She went to schools in South Carolina and Chicago. In 1898 she married Albertus Bethune. In 1904 Bethune started a school for African Americans called the Daytona Normal and Industrial Institute. The school received the support of **Booker T. Washington** (see p. 32). In 1923 Bethune's school was renamed Bethune-Cookman College.

Bethune was president of the National Association of Colored Women from 1924 until 1928. In 1935, she began the National Counsel of Negro Women. From 1936 to 1944 she was President Franklin Roosevelt's special adviser on minority affairs. In 1936 she organized the Federal Council on Negro Affairs. This group also became known as Roosevelt's **"Black Cabinet"** (see below). Bethune served as Director of the Division of Negro Affairs in the National Youth Administration (NYA) from 1939 to 1943. This made her the first African American woman to head a major federal government office. In 1974 a memorial was dedicated to Mary McLeod Bethune in Washington, D.C.

Black Cabinet

The Black Cabinet was the name given to the Federal Council on Negro Affairs, a group of African American advisors to President Franklin Roosevelt in 1936. The group helped to develop government programs for African Americans.

The Black Cabinet

Franklin Roosevelt's Black Cabinet included some of the best-known and civic-minded African Americans of the time. They provided a knowledgeable approach to the many problems of poor African Americans. Some of the members included:

Robert L. Vann, editor of *The Pittsburgh Courier*
William H. Hastie, lawyer, professor at Howard University Law School
Eugene Kinckle Jones, Executive Secretary of the Urban League
Mary McLeod Bethune, educator, President of the National Council of Negro Women
Robert C. Weaver, Harvard economist
Ralph Bunche, professor, Howard University School of Political Science, later won the
    Nobel Peace Prize for work between 1947 and 1949 at the United Nations in settling
    the conflict beween Israel and Palestine
Ted Poston, journalist for the *New York Post*
Crystal Bird Fauset, U.S. Congresswoman, first African American elected to the
    Pennsylvania legislature

Letter Regarding the Brownsville Riots

A group of citizens appealed to Texas governor Lanham for the removal of African American soldiers from their area following the Brownsville Affair (see p. 51). Yet, there was no proof that African Americans had participated in the violence. The following letter is from Judge John Bartlett to Governor Lanham.

"... The Committee of the Citizens of the City have found these facts to exist, after a full and thorough investigation...That about 20 to 25 Negro soldiers, by a concert of action and premeditated plot, broke out of Fort Brown about midnight of August 13th, 1906, and attacked this City, shooting into houses, killing one man, seriously wounding one Police Officer, and wounding one other man.

...We wish to call your attention to the fact that, by means of this unprovoked, wanton and malicious attack upon our people...it is the wish of the entire population of this City that the said Negro soldiers be removed from this place, at the earliest possible time, and replaced by white soldiers before they leave...We would further state that the people here, under the circumstances of the indignity and outrage committed upon them, have conducted themselves in a wonderfully calm and law-abiding manner..."

Source: Texas State Library and Archives Commission

The Black Cabinet helped advise President Roosevelt's **New Deal** (see p. 62). This set of programs promised to assist workers, the unemployed, and all others affected by the Great Depression. Because of the work of the Black Cabinet, the number of African Americans employed by the federal government between 1933 and 1946 rose from 50,000 to almost 200,000.

Brotherhood of Sleeping Car Porters

The Brotherhood of Sleeping Car Porters was the first successful African American–led trade union. The Pullman Company, a railroad company, employed more African Americans than any other corporation. They worked long days for low wages as baggage carriers and ticket takers with no job security. In 1925, an African American activist named A. Phillip Randolph organized the formation of the union to improve conditions (also see **March on Washington Movement**, p. 60).

Brownsville Affair

The Brownsville Affair, also known as the Brownsville Raid, took place on August 13, 1906, in Brownsville, Texas. During a shooting, one white man was killed. A police officer and another white man were wounded. A group of African American soldiers was blamed. It was proven that none of the soldiers had fired his gun. In spite of this, President Theodore Roosevelt dishonorably dismissed 167 African American soldiers. This damaged his reputation as a civil rights advocate among African Americans.

In 1972 the Nixon Administration awarded honorable discharges to each soldier dismissed at Brownsville.

Carver, George Washington

George Washington Carver was born on a plantation in Missouri in 1865. He learned to read and write at home. He became the first African American to attend Iowa State College of Agriculture and Mechanic Arts.

Carver was a leader of the debate team, led the campus military regiment, and had his poetry published in the student newspaper. He also had two of his paintings exhibited at the 1893 World's Fair in Chicago. Yet, his main focus of study was plants.

After finishing his bachelor's degree, Carver stayed at Iowa State College to complete graduate studies in plant breeding. He later became Iowa State College's first African American faculty member. In 1896, **Booker T. Washington** (see p. 32) invited George Washington Carver to join the faculty of Alabama's Tuskegee Institute. Carver encouraged his students to understand how nature affects agriculture. His studies at the Tuskegee Institute brought international recognition to Carver and to the school.

Carver's study of peanuts resulted in over 300 peanut products. Over 100 products resulted from his study of sweet potatoes. Both peanuts and sweet potatoes

George Washington Carver in his laboratory. (Library of Congress)

became alternatives to growing cotton in the South. They also contributed to soil improvement and production. This helped the economic development of farm areas. Among Carver's many creations were adhesives, axle grease, bleach, buttermilk, chili sauce, instant coffee, mayonnaise, meat tenderizer, shampoo, shaving cream, talcum powder, and wood filler.

Carver taught at the Tuskegee Institute for 46 years. During his lifetime he received many awards. He died on January 5, 1943.

Chicago Defender

Robert S. Abbott first published the *Chicago Defender* in 1905. By 1917, it had become the nation's most influential African American newspaper.

The *Chicago Defender* reported events of racial violence. It also encouraged southern blacks to migrate to the North during the **Great Migration** (see p. 57). By 1956 the newspaper had become the largest black-owned daily newspaper in the world.

Cotton Club

The Cotton Club first opened in the mid-1920s in the section of New York City called Harlem. Its owner was Owney Madden, a white gangster. He designed the club to look like a Southern plantation. The Cotton Club was a nightclub. Food and drinks were served and there was entertainment. The entertainers and servers were African American, but there was a "whites only" policy for guests. Some of the best African American entertainers performed at the Cotton Club. These included Duke Ellington, Cab Calloway, Bill "Bojangles" Robinson, Lena Horne, and the Nicholas Brothers.

Drew, Charles Richard

Dr. Charles Richard Drew (1904–1950) was born in Washington, D.C. Dr. Drew received his Doctor of Medicine degree from Columbia University in 1940. He was the first African American to do so. Drew's research lead to the opening of the first blood bank. This was at Presbyterian Hospital in New York City in 1939.

In 1940 Dr. Drew set up a blood bank in London, England to aid the men wounded in **World War II** (see p. 67). His improved ways of collecting and storing blood saved lives. In 1941 Dr. Drew became the first director of the American Red Cross Blood Bank.

In 1941 the U.S. military ordered that blood be separated according to the race of the donor. Blood from African Americans was not allowed to be given to whites. Dr. Drew was against this. He said it was unscientific. He resigned in protest. In 1944 he became chief of surgery at Freedmen's Hospital in Washington, D.C.

For his contributions to science the **National Association for the Advancement of Colored People** (see p. 62) awarded Dr. Drew the Spingarn Medal for outstanding achievement by an African American in 1944. In 1950, after he died, he was awarded the Distinguished Service Medal by the National Medical Association. In 1981 The U.S. Postal Service issued a postage stamp in his honor as part of its "Great Americans" series.

Du Bois, William Edward Burghardt

William Edward Burghardt Du Bois (1868–1963) was one of the most important figures in African American history during the early 20th century. He was born in Great Barrington,

The Souls of Black Folk, 1903

In his book *The Souls of Black Folk*, W.E.B. Du Bois directly criticized Booker T. Washington. Du Bois argued for a unity in establishing full equality for African Americans.

His doctrine has tended to make the whites . . .shift the burden of the Negro problem to the Negro's shoulders and stand aside as critical and rather **pessimistic** spectators; when in fact the burden belongs to the nation, and the hands of none of us are clean if we bend not our energies to righting these great wrongs.... So far as Mr. Washington preaches Thrift, Patience, and Industrial Training.... we must hold up his hands and strive with him.... But so far as Mr. Washington apologizes for injustice . . . does not rightly value the privilege and duty of voting, belittles the . . . effects of **caste** distinctions, and opposes the higher training and ambition of our brighter minds . . . we must unceasingly and firmly oppose [him]. . .

Source: W.E.B. Du Bois, *The Souls of Black Folk*.

◄ **pessimistic**
negative

◄ **caste**
racial category

W. E. B. Du Bois (National Portrait Gallery)

Massachusetts in 1868. Although both of his parents were free, his grandparents on his mother's side had both been enslaved. Du Bois attended Fisk University in Nashville. He said that at this point in his life he "came to a region where the world was split into white and black halves, and where the darker half was held back by race prejudice and legal bonds, as well as by deep ignorance and dire poverty."

Following graduation from Fisk University, Du Bois attended Harvard University. He graduated with honors two years later at the age of 20. Du Bois continued both his masters and doctorate studies at Harvard.

During the late 1890s Du Bois began challenging Booker T. Washington on how African Americans should educate themselves. Washington believed that African Americans should concentrate on schooling themselves in such areas as agriculture and the trades. Du Bois strongly believed African Americans should concentrate on more academic areas.

Du Bois taught at several well-known universities. He was one of the founders of the **Niagara Movement** (see p. 63) as well as a founding member of the **National Association for the Advancement of Colored People** (see p. 62).

In 1903 he wrote his most famous book, *The Souls of Black Folk*. In this book Du Bois argued against segregation. Du Bois called for the establishment of a black elite. This group would be made up of the most educated African Americans. Du Bois referred to them as the "talented ten percent." According to Du Bois, this "Talented Tenth" would win social equality for African Americans because they would be respected by educated whites.

In 1910 Du Bois became the editor of the NAACP's monthly journal, the *Crisis*. By 1918 the journal had over 100,000 subscribers. In 1920 the NAACP awarded Du Bois the Spingarn Medal for his work in promoting civil rights for African Americans.

Between **World War I** (see p. 67) and **World War II** (see p. 67), Du Bois continued to teach and to write books on history and politics. The U.S. Justice Department accused him of being a foreign agent. In 1961 Du Bois joined the Communist Party. He moved to the West African nation of Ghana. He lived there until his death in 1963.

education

Few African American children in the South attended school in the early 1900s. In 1910, 46.6 percent of all black children were working instead of attending school. By 1930 the figure had dropped to 16.1 percent. The **Great Migration** (see p. 57) allowed many African American children to attend school for the first time. Segregation of schools was not allowed in many northern states. However, because there was segregation of housing, schools in black neighborhoods had all black students. Southern states promised African Americans better schools to keep them from moving to the North. Yet, by 1934 only 18 percent of black

"I Will Not Tolerate Any Mixing of the Races"

Army Airforce Major General Frank Hunter's order to the 477th Bombardment Group stationed at Selfridge Field in Michigan. General Hunter gave the following briefing to the 477th Bomber Group upon its arrival in Michigan during the final months of World War II. Later the Group was transferred to Freeman Field in Indiana where they held a protest.

The War Department is not ready to recognize blacks on the level of social equal to white men. This is not the time for blacks to fight for equal rights or personal advantages. They should prove themselves in combat first. There will be no race problem here, for I will not tolerate any mixing of the races. Anyone who protests will be classed as an agitator, sought out, and dealt with accordingly. This is my base and, as long as I am in command, there will be no social mixing of the white and colored officers. The single Officers Club on base will be used solely by white officers. You colored officers will have to wait until an Officers Club is built for your use. Are there any questions? If there are, I will deal with them personally.

Source: National Archives

youth in the South attended high school. The figure for white children in the South was 54 percent.

Freeman Field Mutiny

The Freeman Field Mutiny was a protest by the *Tuskegee Airmen* of the all-black 477th Bomber Group. It happened during **World War II** (see p. 67) at Freeman Field in Indiana.

The airmen protested because the officers' clubs were segregated. Black officers decided to walk into the white officers' club in groups of five and request service. If they were arrested, they would not resist.

By the end of the protest 162 African American officers had been arrested. They refused to sign a statement saying they had read and understood the base segregation order. Later the charges were dropped or the men were found not guilty.

Garvey, Marcus

Marcus Garvey was born in Jamaica. After traveling in South and Central America in his early 20's he was struck by how difficult life was for most people of African descent wherever he traveled. In 1914, he founded the Universal Negro Improvement Association. The goal of the group was to improve conditions for African peoples around the world, and to help in the development of Africa itself. In 1916, he moved to New York City. Once there, he began speaking out in favor of a "Back to Africa" movement in which African Americans and other Africans would move to Africa. In 1925, he was sentenced to 5 years in jail for misusing the U.S. mail in cheating investors in a steamship company he started called Black Star Line. He was *deported*, or forced to leave, from the United States to return to Jamaica, in 1927.

Great Migration

The Great Migration refers to a period between **World War I** (see p. 67) and **World War II** (see p. 67). During this time a great number of African Americans moved from the rural South to the urban North. Times were very difficult for southern blacks in the years before World War I. Cotton crops had been destroyed by a beetle called the boll weevil. In 1910, 90 percent of all African Americans still lived in the South. Eighty percent of those lived in rural areas. The needs of **World War I** (see p. 67) created a great demand for workers in the industrial North. Southern workers earned 50 cents to $2 a day, but northern workers earned from $2 o $5 a day. African Americans headed North with the hope of a new job and of a better life.

Cities such as Chicago, Pittsburgh, and Detroit seemed like the best places to find work. Many southern blacks settled in

"Lots of Work to Be Had"

Newspapers like the *Chicago Defender* encouraged African Americans to move north. Ads were run in the newspaper for mechanics, cement masons, carpenters, painters, bookkeepers, and many other skilled and unskilled workers. This letter to the *Chicago Defender* came from from Port Arthur, Texas, on May 5, 1917.

In reading the *Defender* want ad I notice that there is lots of work to be had and if I havent miscomprehended I think I also understand that the transportation is advanced to able bodied working men is out of work and desire work. Am I not right? With the understanding that those who have been advanced transportation same will be deducted from their salary after they have begun work. Now then if this is they proposition I have about 10 or 15 good working men who is out of work and are dying to leave the South and I assure you that they are working men and will be too glad to come North East or West, any where but the south.

Source: *Chicago Defender*

New York's Harlem section. From 1917 to 1930 almost two million African Americans migrated from the rural South to northern cities. The number of African Americans employed in northern industries increased from about 15 percent in 1910 to about 65 percent in 1930. Thousands of African Americans also migrated west, especially to California. Many more left the rural South to live in southern cities.

Finding housing in northern cities became very difficult for African Americans. They were often charged higher rents. Sometimes they were not allowed to rent property at all. They were also prevented from buying property.

Harlem Renaissance

During the **Great Migration** (see p. 57), many African Americans settled in Harlem. During the 1920s African American writers and musicians gathered in Harlem. Langston Hughes wrote of his arrival in Harlem on a subway train, "I can never put on paper the thrill of the underground ride to Harlem. I went up the steps and out into the bright September sunlight. Harlem! I stood there, dropped my bags, took a deep breath and felt happy again."

The work of talented African American poets, novelists, musicians, and actors coming out of Harlem during the 1920s became known as the Harlem Renaissance. Their contributions to **arts and literature** (see p. 45) created a sense of respect for African culture and pride in being African American. The Harlem Renaissance faded with the beginning of the Great Depression in the 1930s.

Houston Mutiny

In 1917, African American soldiers rebelled against **Jim Crow Laws** (see p. 24) in Houston, Texas. This was called the Houston Mutiny. Sixteen whites and four black soldiers were killed. Nineteen other African American soldiers were court-martialed and executed for their part in the riot. Many other soldiers received long jail sentences. After the Houston Mutiny the war department sent fewer black troops to fight in France in World War I.

Jazz

Jazz first came out of New Orleans, Louisiana at the end of the 19th century. Its roots were in traditional African and African

Key Artists of the Harlem Renaissance

Many African American artists contributed their talents to the Harlem Renaissance. The work of Harlem Renaissance writers, actors, and musicians continued to affect the work of later generations of African American artists. Some Harlem Renaissance artists include:

In literature:	In art:	In music and theater:
Sterling Brown	Aaron Douglas	Count Basie
Countee Cullen	William H. Johnson	Eubie Blake
Jessie Fauset	Sargent Johnson	Duke Ellington
Rudolph Fisher	Lois Mailou Jones	Lillian Evanti
Langston Hughes	Archibald Motley	Fletcher Henderson
Zora Neale Hurston	Horace Pippin	James P. Johnson
Georgia Douglas	Augusta Savage	Rose McClendon
Johnson		Florence Mills
James Weldon Johnson		Paul Robeson
Nella Larsen		Noble Sissle
Alain Locke		William Grant Still
Claude McKay		Ethel Waters
Jean Toomer		

American rhythms as well as in European band music. Jelly Roll Morton (1890–1941) is thought by many to be the first jazz pianist and composer of New Orleans–style jazz music.

Joseph "King" Oliver (1885–1938) was considered the "king of the cornet" in the 1910s. Oliver moved from New Orleans to Chicago in 1918. He was the first African American to introduce New Orleans style jazz to northern audiences. His band was the Creole Jazz Band. In 1922 **Louis Armstrong** (1898–1971) (see p. 47) joined King Oliver's band.

Bessie Smith (1894 – 1937) was a popular blues and jazz singer during the 1920s. She recorded "St. Louis Blues" with Louis Armstrong in 1925.

In 1927 Duke Ellington's band played at New York's famous **Cotton Club** (see p. 52). By this time Ellington, known as the

Bessie Smith (Library of Congress)

"Duke," had become famous for his sophisticated jazz sound. As a bandleader, composer and recording artist, Duke Ellington produced some of the most influential music ever produced. These include, "Mood Indigo," "Down Beat," "Sentimental Lady," and "Swing, Swing, Swing."

March on Washington Movement

In 1941, A. Philip Randolph organized the March on Washington Movement (MOWM). He encouraged 100,000 African Americans to march to Washington, D.C. The purpose of the march was to force the defense industry to provide more jobs for African Americans. The MOWM also wanted the armed forces to be fully integrated. The march was planned for July 1, 1941.

In response to the threatened march, President Roosevelt issued an *executive order*. The order banned racial discrimination in defense industry jobs and in federal employment. It also created the Fair Employment Practices Committee. Randolph cancelled the march on June 28th.

Margold Report

The Margold Report is named for Nathan Ross Margold. He was a white attorney working for the **NAACP** (see p. 62). In 1933, he published a paper that outlined a strategy for countering the idea known as the "separate but equal" doctrine. This idea was that forced segregation was legal as long as separate facilities used by different races were equal. Margold's strategy was to prove that segregated schools were not equal because funding for black schools was so much less than funding for white schools. He argued that such inequity in funding violated the equal protection clause of the 14th Amendment to the Constitution.

After the Margold Report was published, the NAACP used Margold's strategy to battle legal segregation. In 1939 Thurgood Marshall was chief counsel to the NAACP. He used the Margold Report to successfully argue for equal pay for teachers in nine Maryland counties. In its landmark 1954 decision, *Brown v. Board of Education* (see p. 81) the U.S. Supreme Court would end legal segregation, stating that "separate is inherently unequal." The lawyer arguing in favor of desegregation was, once again, Thurgood Marshall of the NAACP. Marshall would later become the first African American on the Supreme Court.

Nation of Islam

The Nation of Islam is a religious movement that takes many of its principles from the Islamic religion. It is also known as the Black Muslim movement. In 1931 Elijah Muhammad (born Robert Poole) met Master Wallace Fard (or Wali Farad), who is considered the founder of the Nation of Islam. Together they opened the Temple of Islam in Detroit. They had about 8,000 followers.

In 1934, the Nation of Islam opened the Temple of Islam Number 2 in Chicago. Other temples were opened in large cities. The message of the leaders of the Nation of Islam is that of racial separation, recognition of a black identity, and economic independence for blacks. During the 1960s, the Nation of Islam would gain national attention due to the powerful personality and leadership of one of its ministers, **Malcolm X** (see p. 87).

National Association for the Advancement of Colored People (NAACP)

The National Association for the Advancement of Colored People (NAACP) was started in 1909 by a group of African Americans and whites, including **W. E. B. Du Bois** (see p. 53) and Joel Spingarn. The NAACP worked for equal rights for African Americans. During its early years the NAACP fought for federal anti-lynching laws. It made the public aware of southern white mob violence. Under the leadership of James Weldon Johnson, membership in the NAACP grew from 9,282 in 1917 to 91,203 in 1919. By 1935 the NAACP had over 325 branches located in almost every state.

negro leagues

African American baseball club owners met in February 1920 to form the Negro National League. It broke up in 1931. In 1937 the Negro American League was formed to replace it. African American baseball teams played each other. Among the stars of the negro leagues are pitcher Satchel Paige, outfielder James "Cool Papa" Bell, and catcher Josh Gibson. The negro leagues closed during the early 1950s after **Jackie Robinson** (see p. 91) helped desegregate the major leagues.

New Deal

In 1933 President Franklin D. Roosevelt launched the New Deal. The New Deal was the name given to a group of federal programs aimed at helping Americans recover from Great Depression. Its purpose was to rebuild the American economy and to put people back to work.

Two programs of the New Deal, the Works Progress Administration (WPA) and the Agricultural Adjustment Administration (AAA), had a direct impact on African

Americans. Over 5,000 African American teachers worked for the WPA's education programs. The WPA employed several black artists, musicians, and writers to perform and work with African American children. However, the WPA did not treat African American employees equally.

One of the policies of the AAA was to pay farmers to not grow crops. The idea was that if the supply of crops fell, prices would increase. This would benefit the farmers. The policy was a disaster for sharecroppers and **tenant farmers**. Since landowners would be paid not to grow crops, they wanted to evict the tenant farmers from the land, since they no longer needed them to grow crops.

In 1934 the Southern Tenant Farmers' Union formed to fight the eviction of black and white tenants and sharecroppers. By 1935 over 10,000 farmers had joined the union.

Niagara Movement

The Niagara Movement was organized in 1905 to challenge the ideas of **Booker T. Washington** (see p. 32). Led by **W. E. B.**

"Declaration of Principles" by W. E. B. Du Bois

The "Declaration of Principles" became the guide for the Niagara Movement. It called for civil rights and equality in education, employment, health, and all other areas affected by social injustice.

Education: Common school education should be free to all American children and compulsory...

Courts: We demand upright judges in courts, juries selected without discrimination on account of color and the same measure of punishment...for black as for white offenders...

'Jim Crow' Cars: We protest against the 'Jim Crow' car, since its effect is and must be to make us pay first-class fare for third-class accommodations...

Soldiers: We regret that his nation has never seen fit adequately to reward the black soldiers who, in its five wars, have defended their country with their blood, and yet have been systematically denied the promotions which their abilities deserve. And we regard as unjust, the exclusion of black boys from the military and naval training schools...

Source: W.E.B. Du Bois Library, University of Massachusetts, Amherst

Chicago Daily Journal, July 29, 1919

News accounts in the Chicago papers told of the mob violence during Red Summer. This story tells of the pursuit of a lone African American by an enraged white mob.

Negro Fights. . . Against Crowd in Loop, Shot When He Ceases Running to Battle Whites Second Time

A lone Negro, evidently on his way home from work in the loop at 6 a.m., was shot to death near the corner of Wabash Avenue and Adams Street after he had failed in a helpless, desperate fight to escape from the mob of white men who bore down upon him.

The crowd was driven early in the morning from the streets of the black belt, where they had passed a rageful night. The mob marched north in Michigan Avenue shouting, brandishing clubs, baseball bats, occasionally shooting revolvers. The avenue was free of any Negro victims.

The procession turned west on Adams Street. They spied their victim on the corner of Wabash Avenue. The Negro, warned by their howling threats, ran south. He threw away his hat and coat as he fled, a score of white men, wildly running after him...

Source: *Chicago Daily Journal*

Du Bois (see p. 53), the Niagara Movement became the first organized African American protest movement of the 20th century. Several of its members helped form the **National Association for the Advancement of Colored People (NAACP)** in 1909 (see p. 62).

Red Summer

The **Great Migration** (see p. 57) had brought thousands of African Americans to live in cities. This created competition between whites and blacks for jobs and housing. Violence resulted in the summer of 1919.

There were 26 major race riots. Hundreds of people were killed or injured. Most of them were African Americans. The worst rioting took place in Chicago. The rioting there lasted for 13 days. Thirty people were killed and over 500 were injured. Property damage left about 1000 African Americans homeless. African American leaders termed the time Red (meaning "bloody") Summer.

The SCOTTSBORO BOYS MUST NOT DIE!

MASS SCOTTSBORO DEFENSE MEETING

At St. Mark's M. E. Church
137th Street and St. Nicholas Avenue

Friday Eve., April 14th, 8 P. M.

Protest the infamous death verdict rendered by an all-white jury at Decatur, Alabama against HAYWOOD PATTERSON

The Meeting will be addressed by:

Mrs. JANIE PATTERSON, mother of Haywood Patterson, victim of the lynch verdict; SAMUEL LEIBOWITZ, chief counsel for the defense; JOSEPH BRODSKY, defense counsel, WILLIAM PATTERSON, National Secretary of the I. L. D.; RICHARD B. MOORE, Dr. LORENZO KING, WM. KELLEY of the Amsterdam News, and others.

THUNDER YOUR INDIGNATION AGAINST THE JUDICIAL MURDER OF INNOCENT NEGRO CHILDREN!

COME TO THE MASS PROTEST MEETING

AT ST. MARK'S M. E. CHURCH
137th Street and St. Nicholas Avenue

FRIDAY EVENING, APRIL 14th, 8 P. M.

A poster advertising a public meeting to organize a defense for the accused African American young men during the Scottsboro Boys trial. (Library of Congress)

Scottsboro Boys

On March 25, 1931, nine African American youths, ages 12 to 20, were arrested near Scottsboro, Alabama. They were charged with assaulting two white women. A trial was set for six days later. Alabama law required the judge to appoint a lawyer for the boys. The judge did not do this. On the day of the case, two lawyers said that they would defend the accused youths. The judge gave the lawyers 30 minutes to prepare their case. Eight of the nine defendants were convicted and sentenced to death. The court's decision was appealed to the U.S. Supreme Court where it was overturned. In *Powell* v. *Alabama*, the Supreme Court ruled

Powell v. Alabama (1932)

In a 7–2 decision, the U.S. Supreme Court overturned the convictions of the nine defendants in the Scottsboro Boys Case based on the due process clause of the 14th Amendment. As the result of this decision, states were required to provide legal counsel for poor defendants in all cases where the death penalty could be imposed.

In the light of the facts outlined in...this opinion—the ignorance and illiteracy of the defendants, their youth, the circumstances of public hostility, the imprisonment and the close surveillance of the defendants by the military forces, the fact that their friends and families were all in other states and communication with them necessarily difficult, and above all that they stood in deadly peril of their lives—we think the failure of the trial court to give them reasonable time and opportunity to secure counsel was a clear denial of due process...

Source: National Archives

that the boys had been denied their right to a fair trial. It based its decision on the 14th Amendment.

Alabama retried the Scottsboro Boys and again found them guilty. In *Norris* v. *Alabama* (1935) the U.S. Supreme Court once again overturned the convictions. This time the convictions were found unconstitutional because African Americans had been excluded from the jury.

They were tried and convicted for a third time. It was not until 1950 that the last defendant was released from prison on parole.

Tulsa Riot

The Tulsa Riot was one of the worst race riots of the 20th century. It started with the planned lynching of an African American by a white mob. During the attempt a white man was shot. This began the riot. The entire section of Tulsa's prosperous Greenwood district, also known as "black Wall Street," was destroyed. Whites set fire to homes and businesses and shot African Americans at will. Hundreds of African Americans were killed.

Today only one block remains of the original Greenwood District destroyed in the 1921 Tulsa Riot.

World War I

During World War I (1917–1919), African Americans tried to end segregation in the military. They saw service in World War I as a way to be granted full civil rights. However, this did not happen.

In 1917 almost 400,000 African Americans were drafted into military service. Most of them served in non-combat positions. However, 40,000 served in two all-black divisions. The 369th Infantry served in the French combat zone under French command. They were the first American soldiers to cross the Rhine River. The 369th served 191 continuous days in combat, the longest of any American Unit. Henry Johnson and Needham Roberts of the 369th received France's highest medal, the Croix de Guerre (*cro-AH duh gare*) for their bravery in battle.

Among the all–African American groups serving in World War I was the 15th New York Regiment. The unknown soldier in this paintng was a member of that force. (West Point Museum)

World War II

The Selective Service and Training Act of 1940 outlawed "discrimination against any person on account of race or color." In spite of this, discrimination and segregation continued throughout the armed forces. However, after the United States entered World War II (1939–1945) in 1941, slow changes did take place.

Benjamin O. Davis, Sr. became the first African American to become a brigadier general. Also, before World War II, the armed forces accepted only white women as nurses. During the war the Army and the Navy accepted a few African American women as nurses.

In July 1941 African American pilots began training at segregated facilities at Tuskegee Institute. They became known as the *Tuskegee Airmen*. The 450 Tuskegee Airmen flew over fifteen thousand missions, protected U.S. bombers on 200 bombing missions over Germany, and shot down or damaged over 400 enemy aircraft. On March 15th, 1945, they received a Presidential Unit Citation.

Dorie Miller Wins the Navy Cross Medal

On May 27, 1942 the Navy awarded the Navy Cross to Doris (Dorie) Miller for heroism during the December 7, 1941, Japanese attack on Pearl Harbor. An enemy submarine sank his assigned ship, the Liscome Bay, in 1943. He was killed and was awarded the Purple Heart. His Navy Cross citation read:

For services set forth in the following:

CITATION: "For distinguished devotion to duty, extraordinary courage and disregard for his own personal safety during the attack on the Fleet in Pearl Harbor, Territory of Hawaii, by Japanese forces on December 7, 1941. While at the side of his Captain on the bridge, Miller, despite enemy strafing and bombing and in the face of a serious fire, assisted in moving his Captain, who had been mortally wounded, to a place of greater safety, and later manned and operated a machine gun directed at enemy Japanese attacking aircraft until ordered to leave the bridge."

Source: National Archives

Segregated all-black infantry units fought in Italy and France. Several African Americans won medals. Private Ernest A. Jenkins received a Silver Star for bravery from General George S. Patton on October 13, 1944.

African Americans took part in the D-Day landing on the coast of France on August 18, 1944. One African American private, Warren Capers, set up a medical station. He treated more than 330 soldiers on that day alone.

The Navy also segregated African Americans. Entire naval vessels, including the USS *Mason* and PC 1264, were staffed by African Americans. On June 3, 1944, the all-black USS *Harriet Tubman* was launched.

Segregation in the armed forces officially ended in 1948 by President Harry Truman. His order called for equality in the armed forces. However, it would be several years before the armed forces were fully integrated.

CHAPTER THREE

We Shall Overcome

The Civil Rights Era, 1946-1968

"For years now I have heard the word 'Wait!' It rings in the ear of every Negro with piercing familiarity. This 'Wait' has almost always meant 'Never.' We must come to see, with one of our distinguished jurists, that "justice too long delayed is justice denied."

—Martin Luther King, Jr., "Letter from a Birmingham Jail," 1963

After **World War II** (see p. 67), African Americans were more determined than ever not to be second-class citizens. Returning soldiers and their families were no longer willing to accept excuses.

The war's end left the United States in a new rivalry with the Soviet Union. It was called the Cold War because open warfare never broke out. Each nation published *propaganda* to attack the other. The Russians claimed that American treatment of African Americans made its claims of freedom and justice a lie. This argument won over countries where people of color struggled against white colonial rulers.

President Harry Truman pointed this out in his efforts to promote social justice. In 1948, he sent a special message to Congress calling for the protection of every citizen's civil rights. Congress made no response.

Democrat Truman was narrowly elected president. He defeated Republican Thomas Dewey and two other smaller party candidates. One was Progressive Henry Wallace and the other was Dixiecrat Strom Thurmond. Wallace wanted total equality for blacks while Thurmond strongly opposed Truman's proposals. In 1950, Truman banned racial discrimination in civil service positions. He also ended segregation in the armed forces. The first integrated troops served in the Korean War.

DESEGREGATION AT SCHOOL AND ELSEWHERE

Truman's successor was former General Dwight D. Eisenhower. He was not a strong civil rights advocate. However, civil rights leaders were not going to wait for the government to set things right. Membership in the **National Association for the Advancement of Colored People (NAACP)** (see p. 62) was at an all-time high. The group put much money and energy into legal challenges to segregation.

In 1954 the Supreme Court ruled against school desegregation in *Brown v. Board of Education* (see p. 81). Lawyer **Thurgood Marshall** (see p. 89) had argued the case successfully. African Americans were joyful. In reality, it took more than a decade to end the "separate but equal" schools that had been permitted by *Plessy v. Ferguson* (see p. 26).

African Americans also wanted to integrate other places. They began "sit-ins." Blacks and whites simply sat together in a place that was restricted to whites only. The **Congress of Racial Equality (CORE)** (see p. 82), led by James Farmer and Bayard Rustin, staged the first **sit-in** (see p. 92). They did this in Chicago restaurants in 1947. In 1947, CORE also organized the first **Freedom Ride** (see p. 82). The goal was to integrate buses in the South. The riders were quickly jailed.

Timeline

1946

Jackie Robinson becomes the first African American to play for major league baseball.

1952

Malcolm X is released from prison. While in jail, he was introduced to the **Nation of Islam**. In time, he will become minister of Temple No. 2, in New York's Harlem.

THE RISE OF MARTIN LUTHER KING, JR.

In 1955, Rosa Parks (see **Montgomery Bus Boycott**, p. 90), a 42-year-old seamstress, struck another blow for civil rights. She sat in the "white" section on a Montgomery, Alabama bus. Parks claimed that she was tired after a long day's work and didn't feel like obeying the white driver's order to move. But her action was deliberate. She was secretary of the local NAACP. The group opposed bus segregation. Parks was arrested and jailed.

After her arrest a large group met to decide what to do. A young Atlanta Baptist minister named **Martin Luther King, Jr.** (see p. 84) addressed them. He had earned a *doctorate* at Boston University. He had studied Christian *theology* and Indian leader Mahatma Gandhi's philosophy of *nonviolent resistance*. King told the crowd of 2,000: "We have known humiliation, we have known abusive language, we have been plunged into the abyss of oppression. And we decided to raise up only with the weapon of protest. It is one of the greatest glories of America that we have the right to protest."

The group decided to stop using the Montgomery buses in protest. The Montgomery *boycott* faced resistance. One hundred of its leaders were charged with crimes, and some went to jail. Four black churches and King's home were bombed. No one gave in. The boycott lasted almost a year. In November 1956, the Supreme Court outlawed segregation in public buses.

1954	1955–1956	1957	1957
Brown v. Board of Education outlaws school segregation.	Montgomery Bus Boycott continues for 381 days.	President Eisenhower sends federal troops to integrate schools in Little Rock, Arkansas.	Southern Christian Leadership Conference (SCLC) is founded by Martin Luther King, Jr. and others. It becomes one of the nation's leading civil rights groups.

King's message reached the hearts and minds of blacks as well as whites. Soon his voice would be one of the most familiar in the last half of the 20th century. In 1956, he led a prayer pilgrimage of 25,000 people to the Lincoln Memorial. The following year, he and the Reverend Ralph Abernathy formed the **Southern Christian Leadership Conference (SCLC)** (see p. 92).

President Eisenhower became a friend of civil rights in spite of himself. He appointed California's Republican governor Earl Warren Chief Justice of the Supreme Court. He later regretted that Warren was so active in the struggle for civil rights. In 1957, Eisenhower sent federal troops into **Little Rock**, Arkansas, (see p. 85) to ensure the protection of nine black students who were integrating Central High School. Later, Congress passed its first civil rights bill since **Reconstruction** (see Vol. 1, p. 123). It set up voting rights safeguards and a civil rights commission to study the issue of racial discrimination. The commission was also charged with recommending actions to Congress. In 1961, the group released a report documenting the effects of segregation. The report would help pave the way for the **Civil Rights Act of 1964** (see p. 82).

THE MOMENTUM BUILDS

To civil rights activists, change had only begun. In 1958, the NAACP organized sit-ins (see p. 92) at lunch counters in Oklahoma City. In 1960, African American college students staged a sit-in at a Greensboro, North Carolina lunch counter. The city then integrated all its eating places. This caused sit-ins to be organized

1960	1960–1961	1962	1963
Student Nonviolent Coordinating Committee (SNCC) is established by young African American activists. The group will participate in major civil rights campaigns like voter registration and the **Freedom Rides**.	Protesters hold sit-ins and **Freedom Rides** throughout the South.	James Meredith, an African American, forces integration at the University of Mississippi.	**Martin Luther King, Jr.** helps organize protests in **Birmingham, Alabama**.

in 100 more cities. Over the next 12 months, 50,000 people took part in sit-ins across the South. Most of the people were black, but some were white.

In 1960, Senator John F. Kennedy of Massachusetts was elected president. Kennedy was the first Catholic president. Because Catholics had also faced discrimination, Kennedy's election raised hopes that civil rights would be an important item on the national agenda.

Matters were more complicated than they seemed. Both Democrats and Republicans were divided between liberals and conservatives. The liberals favored civil rights and the conservatives opposed them. Southern Democrats were conservative and powerful. Kennedy was often in the middle of a party fight. He resisted integration of public housing funded by the federal government. He appointed five judges who opposed integration.

Integration of interstate travel—buses, trains, airplanes and on highways—had long been the law, but never enforced. CORE and the newly organized **Student Nonviolent Coordinating Committee (SNCC)** (see p. 93) decided to challenge this. They organized Freedom Rides in which blacks and whites sat together. In 1961 CORE riders were attacked in South Carolina and in Alabama. Local police and FBI agents watched, but did not stop the attacks. The Nashville-based SNCC group was arrested in **Birmingham, Alabama** (see p. 77) and sent back to Tennessee. They returned to Birmingham and travelled to Montgomery, where whites with clubs attacked them. Soon they were on their way to Jackson, Mississippi. The worldwide media was alerted. Attorney

1963	**1964**	**1964**	**1964**
Martin Luther King, Jr. delivers his "I Have A Dream" speech during the **March on Washington**.	**SNCC** and other groups register voters during **Freedom Summer**.	A major riot breaks out in New York City's Harlem. It was prompted by the shooting of a young boy by police.	Congress passes the **Civil Rights Act of 1964**.

General Robert Kennedy demanded that they be jailed in Jackson to protect them from mob violence.

In September 1962 African American James Meredith integrated the University of Mississippi. President Kennedy sent 12,000 troops to protect him. In the spring of 1962 George Wallace, Governor of Alabama, tried to defy an order to integrate the University of Alabama. Kennedy's Justice Department stood up to Wallace.

DEMONSTRATIONS FACE RESISTANCE

Throughout the Deep South there were demonstrations in support of black voters and the right to use public facilities. Thousands of blacks and some whites faced police clubs, tear gas, attack dogs and high-powered hoses. The demonstrations were common on national news, but often ignored locally. In just three months of 1963, the Justice Department took note of 1,400 sit-ins.

White challenges to integration ranged from violence to quiet resistance. Civil rights groups did not agree on how to react. Roy Wilkins led the **NAACP** (see p. 62). He thought Martin Luther King, Jr. and the SCLC were provoking danger. CORE was largely a city organization. SNCC took on oppression in the rural South. Each group, naturally, thought its own work was most important.

SNCC worked to register voters in Greenwood, Mississippi. The SCLC worried about how to confront Birmingham. That city was the hardcore center

1964	**1965**	**1965**	**1965**
Martin Luther King, Jr. wins the Nobel Peace Prize.	After activists attempting to march from Selma to Montgomery, Alabama to support voting rights are beaten by police, civil rights supporters from around the nation arrive in Alabama to complete a second march.	Lyndon Johnson signs the **Voting Rights Act of 1965**, making it illegal to deny qualified voter the right to vote based on their race.	**Malcolm X** is assassinated.

of segregation. There, on Easter weekend, King and Abernathy led a small group who defied a police order not to demonstrate. King and his followers were jailed. While in jail, King read a newspaper notice from white *clergymen* asking him to back down. King became angry with this. In the margins of the paper, he began his famous "Letter from a Birmingham Jail." In it he explained his convictions and expressed his frustration with white "moderates."

King left jail feeling let down. At that point James Bevel energized the Birmingham movement. He was an SNCC member who wanted to mobilize the city's young people. Although many criticized King for permitting it, in May, hundreds of children marched and were sent to jail. They were attacked by police dogs and streams of water from fire hoses. The whole world seemed to react to this. Finally, Birmingham was forced to desegregate its lunch counters and dressing rooms. That same year, white supremacists bombed a Birmingham church and killed four young black girls.

In August 1963, civil rights groups overcame their differences. They joined to stage a civil rights **March on Washington** (see p. 89). As the crowd of perhaps 200,000 gathered from all over the nation, King set the tone for the march in his "I Have a Dream" speech. The crowd left peacefully.

VIOLENCE TRIUMPHS

The march may have been the most peaceful moment in the civil rights movement. That November, John F. Kennedy was assassinated. President Lyndon

1966	**1968**	**1968**	**1968**
The **Black Panther Party** is formed. Frustrated by the slow pace of the civil rights movement, the more radical group argues that African Americans should defend their rights with force if needed.	**Martin Luther King, Jr.** begins planning for a multiracial "Poor People's Campaign" to protest against poverty.	**Martin Luther King, Jr.,** is assassinated.	The **Black Panther Party** joins the **Black Power** movement.

Johnson pressured Congress to pass the 1964 **Civil Rights Act** (see p. 82) and the Equal Opportunity Act. Martin Luther King Jr. won international recognition with the Nobel Peace Prize. However, African Americans grew angrier.

A new leader, **Malcolm X** (see p. 87), began to draw attention. He rejected nonviolent Christianity for a *separatist* Black Muslim faith. Riots broke out in New York City when the Mississippi Freedom Democratic Party failed to unseat the all-white delegation from that state.

King led a successful, but bloody march from Selma to Montgomery. Three demonstrators were killed. Shortly after this, Black Muslim rivals killed Malcolm X. Thirty-four more people died in riots in the Watts section of Los Angeles. SNCC's new chair, Stokely Carmichael, proclaimed "Black Power." He announced that whites were no longer welcome to join SNCC. The revolutionary **Black Panther Party** (see p. 79) was formed in Oakland, California.

Forces larger than Martin Luther King seemed to be taking over. Neither new civil rights legislation nor the appointment of NAACP lawyer Thurgood Marshall to the U.S. Supreme Court as the first African American justice could stop the rioting that broke out in black neighborhoods in 75 cities. In 1968, when King himself was assassinated, more cities burst into flame. That year, the Kerner Commission was created to study the matter. It blamed discrimination and poverty for black rage and rioting.

1968 · 1968 · 1968

Arthur Ashe becomes the first African American to win the U.S. Open men's singles championship.

Alabama governor **George Wallace** runs as an independent candidate, winning five Southern states. He promises to continue segregation policies.

Two African American athletes, Tommie Smith and John Carlos, raise their fists in a **Black Power** salute while receiving their medals at the 1968 Summer Olympics.

A-Z of Key People, Events, and Terms

Birmingham, Alabama

Birmingham, Alabama was possibly the most segregated city in the United States in 1963. Six years before, 18 unsolved bombings in African American neighborhoods had earned the city the nickname "Bombingham."

Members of the African American community in Birmingham invited **Martin Luther King Jr.** (see p. 84) and the **Southern Christian Leadership Conference (SCLC)** (see p. 92) to their city. Together they decided on a way to protest segregation in the city. In April King and the SCLC staged boycotts against stores that refused to hire African Americans. Then they planned a huge nonviolent march. The protesters met head-to-head with Eugene "Bull" Connor, Birmingham's police commissioner. Connor supported segregation and vowed to uphold it. He got a federal court order barring demonstrations.

King and his followers were ready. Marchers prepared themselves to be arrested. They believed that if enough of them were arrested, the city's jails would be filled with innocent people. King felt that this would embarrass the mayor and other city officials, forcing them to take a stand against segregation.

At first, Connor arrested a few protesters and the marches mover forward peacefully. Then Martin Luther King, Jr., began to march with the demonstrators. Connor put King and many others into jail. From his jail cell, King wrote his famous "Letter from a Birmingham Jail."

After a time, the arrests and the abuse were taking their toll. Funds were running low from bailing out jailed people. African American ministers and business people began asking King to call off the demonstration. Other leaders tried to convince King to allow children to march. After much debate, it was decided to let the children march.

On May 2, 1963, thousands of school-age children—some as young as six—met at the Sixteenth Street Baptist Church to begin

Birmingham police used attack dogs and high-pressure fire hoses on nonviolent protestors and bystanders. (Library of Congress)

a march. Even before the march began, hundreds of children were taken to jail on that first day. The following day, more children took part in the march. Connor decided to use full force on the children. He directed his police force to use water hoses, cattle prods, and police dogs to attack the nonviolent, unarmed protesters. Television cameras and newspaper reporters recorded unbelievable scenes of horror as attack dogs bit into children's arms and legs and police beat young protesters with clubs. High-pressure hoses, strong enough to strip bark off a tree, were used to push children back. Children were hauled off to jail in police wagons and school buses.

Finally, the federal government took action. President John F. Kennedy sent federal troops to surround Birmingham. The President had negotiators meet with the SCLC, Birmingham's officials and business people. On May 7, 1963 an agreement was reached. The SCLC ended the demonstrations and in exchange the white leaders of Birmingham agreed to desegregate in planned stages. Still, peaceful desegregation would be difficult. The night the negotiation was announced, bombs were thrown at King's motel room and at his brother's home. This started more protests that could have led to violence. A last-minute negotiation between local leaders avoided the danger. Nevertheless, Birmingham would never be the same again.

Black Panther Party (BPP)

The Black Panther Party was one of the most active and radical forces in the struggle for equality during the 1960s. Dressed in black jackets and black berets, the Panthers held marches and demonstrations in many cities to protest segregation and discrimination.

Huey Newton and Bobby Seale founded the BPP in 1966, in Oakland, California. The party's platform included the statement that African Americans wanted nothing more than "land, bread, housing, education, clothing, justice, and peace." The BPP was founded at the height of the Vietnam War. The group demanded that African Americans be exempt from military service. A higher percentage of African Americans were being sent into combat than whites. The BPP wanted this to stop. Another major issue for the BPP was police stopping brutality against members of the African American community. The Black Panthers were influenced by the ideas of **Malcolm X** (see p. 87) and the **Black Power** (see p. 80) movement. The BPP supported the use of self-defense to protect the rights of African Americans. More moderate civil rights groups did not agree with this. However, the group's philosophy appealed to younger African Americans. These young people were frustrated at the slow pace of integration and civil rights legislation.

The Black Panthers believed that African Americans should ban together for a common cause. The group was critical of middle- and upper-class African Americans who refused to help poorer blacks. The Panthers also believed that if African Americans could not get jobs, they should take over white-owned businesses.

In May 1967, the Black Panthers protested a proposed law against carrying loaded weapons in public. After Bobby Seale read a statement, the police arrested him and 30 others. News coverage publicized the event. After this, Black Panther chapters opened around the country.

Later that year, Huey Newton was arrested on charges of murdering a police officer. Another Panther member, Eldridge

Cleaver, organized a "Free Huey" campaign. Cleaver and Seale convinced Stokely Carmichael of the **Student Nonviolent Coordinating Committee (SNCC)** (see p. 93) to join the Panthers. He spoke out on behalf of Newton. Eventually, in 1970, Newton's conviction was overturned and he was freed.

Throughout the late 1960s, tensions between blacks and whites grew. BPP members were arrested. They were accused of carrying and using weapons. The Panthers said the police were arresting them without evidence. In time SNCC and the BPP split. This was over the alliances with white organizations. Stokely Carmichael believed these prevented African Americans from becoming self-reliant.

After his release from prison in 1970, Newton tried to revive the Panthers. Seale ran for mayor of Oakland to try to strengthen the BPP. He lost, but won 40 percent of the votes. By the late 1970s, the Black Panther Party was no longer a political force.

Black Power

Stokely Carmichael was a leader of the **Student Nonviolent Coordinating Committee (SNCC)** (see p. 93). In 1965 he was leading civil rights marchers through Mississippi. "We been saying freedom for six years, and we ain't got nothin'," said Carmichael. "What we gonna start saying now is 'Black Power!'"

Members of the Black Panthers march in New York City in 1970.
(New York Public Library)

Along with Carmichael, the crowd started chanting "Black Power! Black Power!"

Carmichael said Black Power was, "a call for black people to unite, to recognize their heritage, to build a sense of community." He thought African Americans should set goals and lead organizations without help from whites. Black Power was a reaction to years of being beaten during nonviolent protests. Now, African Americans wanted to fight back.

The news media criticized Black Power. African American organizations such as the **National Association for the Advancement of Colored People (NAACP)** (see p. 62) and the **Southern Christian Leadership Conference (SCLC)** (see p. 92) also disagreed with leaving whites out of the Civil Rights Movement. Yet, from 1966 to 1969, many SNCC and **Congress of Racial Equality (CORE)** (see p. 82) members were supporters of Black Power. In 1968, the **Black Panther Party** (see p. 79) joined the Black Power movement.

The Black Power movement was also a cultural movement. It led to college students demanding courses in **African American studies** (see p. 105). They also wanted separate cultural facilities and separate dormitories.

The movement led many African Americans identify with Africa. During the 1960s, many African nations were winning independence after years of colonial rule. Some supporters of Black Power encouraged Pan-Africanism. This was the political and cultural unity of all people of African origin.

Brown v. Board of Education

In this 1954 case the Supreme Court ruled that segregation in public schools was unconstitutional. The case that came before the Supreme Court was several cases put together. All involved segregation of public schools.

Attorneys **Thurgood Marshall** (see p. 89) and Charles Houston argued that segregation in schools went against 14th Amendment. The 14th Amendment guarantees that all citizens are equally protected by the law. The Court agreed. This reversed the *Plessy v. Ferguson* (see p. 26) decision which declared segregation legal if public facilities were "separate but equal." While African Americans celebrated the Court's decision, most realized that integrating all-white

Brown v. Board of Education (1954)

In the Brown case the Supreme Court ruled against segregation in education and overturned *Plessy* v. *Ferguson*. The case, argued by Thurgood Marshall and other NAACP attorneys, was a huge victory for the African American community. Below is a quote from the ruling.

To separate [those children] from others of similar age and qualifications solely because of their race generates a feeling in the community that may affect their hearts and minds in a way unlikely ever to be undone. Separate educational facilities are inherently unequal. Any language in Plessy v. Ferguson contrary to these findings is rejected.

Source: National Archives

schools was going to be extremely difficult. (see **Little Rock**, p. 85).

Some of the difficulty came from the Court's order to desegregate the schools "with all deliberate speed." To African Americans "all deliberate speed" meant as soon as possible. To southern whites, "all deliberate speed" was a vague term, allowing them to take their time.

Civil Rights Act of 1964

The Civil Rights Act of 1964 ended **Jim Crow laws** (see p. 24) in the South. The law ended segregation in public places and made discrimination in employment illegal. The Civil Rights Act also benefited women and other minority groups. It took about six months to push the bill through Congress. President Lyndon Johnson used his connections and his keen sense of politics to do so.

Congress of Racial Equality (CORE)

James Farmer founded CORE in Chicago 1942. This group used non-violent direct action. CORE tried to integrate Chicago's buses and public areas. It is best known for the **Freedom Rides** (see below). It was also involved with voter registration and community issues. In 1999 CORE had about 100,000 members nationwide. It is still active today.

Freedom Rides

The Freedom rides took place in 1961 and 1962. The **Congress of Racial Equality (CORE)** (see above) organized them. Freedom riders were testing a court order to desegregate interstate buses. Groups of six or seven black and white riders would board interstate buses and sit together. When the buses reached the Deep South trouble began. Angry whites would gather outside the bus. They dragged out the freedom riders and beat them. One bus was firebombed.

The Council of Federated Organizations

The Council of Federated Organizations was created by four of the leading civil rights organizations. Its purpose was to register African American voters during the summer of 1964. The organizations that founded the group are listed below:

Name	Date Founded
National Association for the Advancement of Colored People (NAACP)	1909
Congress of Racial Equality (CORE)	1942
Southern Christian Leadership Conference (SCLC)	1957
Student Nonviolent Coordinating Committee (SNCC)	1960

Yet, the freedom rides continued. When a bus organized by the Student Nonviolent Coordinating Committee (SNCC) arrived in **Birmingham, Alabama** (see p. 77), the riders were beaten by police. After being sent back to Tennessee the freedom riders boarded another bus and headed for Montgomery. Once again, they were beaten. Some riders were left bleeding and unconscious.

National attention caused President Kennedy to act. Federal marshals rode with the freedom riders. They enforced the integration laws. The government passed more regulations pressuring local communities to enforce the laws. However, resistance to integration continued.

Freedom Summer

The summer of 1964 is often referred to as "Freedom Summer." Thousands of volunteers travelled from the North to work with volunteers from the South to register voters across the Deep South.

During the summer of 1964, three volunteers, Andrew Goodman, James Chaney, and Michael Schwerner (left to right, above) were killed by members of the Ku Klux Klan for their work registering African Americans to vote. (Library of Congress)

About 1,000 African American and white volunteers were sent to Mississippi alone. The local police and the Ku Klux Klan (sometimes the same people) terrorized the volunteers.

In June, three volunteers—one African American and two whites—disappeared in Mississippi. In August, they were found dead in a swamp. The FBI charged 20 men with conspiracy and 7 Klansmen with the murders. It took three years of trials and appeals to get the men convicted.

In spite of the violence, volunteers managed to register thousands of African Americans.

King, Martin Luther, Jr.

Martin Luther King, Jr. was born in Atlanta, Georgia in 1929. He grew up in a very religious Baptist family. Both his grandfather and his father were ministers. His family was also active in the community. His grandfather had led a protest to get the first African American high school in Atlanta.

King entered Morehouse College at 15 years old. He earned his Ph.D. from Boston University at age 26. Soon after graduation, he and his wife Coretta Scott King moved to Alabama.

King became well known during the **Montgomery Bus Boycott** (see p. 90). He was a strong leader. He and Ralph Abernathy formed the **Southern Christian Leadership Conference (SCLC)** (see p. 92) with nearly 100 other church leaders. King then moved to Atlanta, Georgia, where he served as president of the SCLC and as a part-time minister.

In April 1963, King led demonstrations in **Birmingham, Alabama** (see p. 77), demanding desegregation. Then in August that same year, King took part in the **March on Washington** (see p. 89). There he delivered his famous "I Have a Dream" speech.

The next year, King was awarded the Nobel Peace Prize for his efforts to win racial equality. King eventually came to believe that poverty was the main enemy. King began planning a new movement that he called the Poor People's Campaign. He was going to organize a huge march on Washington to start the campaign in April 1968. On April 3, he delivered a speech in Memphis. He told the crowd, "I've been to the mountaintop, [and] I've seen the glory." King told listeners, "I may not get there with you, but I want you to know that we as a people will get to the Promised Land."

Martin Luther King, Jr. (Library of Congress)

The following day King was shot dead on the balcony of his hotel room. His assassin was James Earl Ray, a white petty criminal who had escaped from prison in 1967.

African Americans became very angry. Riots broke out in 125 cities, leaving 45 dead. President Johnson begged people to stay calm, but the riots continued. With Martin Luther King, Jr. gone, the civil rights movement would take a different turn.

Little Rock, desegregation of

In 1954, the Supreme Court ordered desegregation of schools in *Brown v. Board of Education* (see p. 81). The African American community, however, was anxious to put the ruling to the test.

President Eisenhower on Desegregation, 1957

When the Little Rock school district refused to integrate, President Dwight D. Eisenhower issued Executive Order 10730 to enforce the law. In an address to the nation, he explained why he issued the order.

In that city, under the leadership of . . . extremists, disorderly mobs have deliberately prevented the carrying out of proper orders from a federal court. Local authorities have not eliminated that violent opposition and, under the law, I yesterday issued a proclamation calling upon the mob to disperse.

This morning the mob again gathered in front of the Central High School of Little Rock, obviously for the purpose of again preventing the carrying out of the court's order relating to the admission of Negro children to that school.

Whenever normal agencies prove inadequate to the task and it becomes necessary for the Executive Branch of the federal government to use its powers and authority to uphold federal courts, the President's responsibility is inescapable. In accordance with that responsibility, I have today issued an executive order directing the use of troops under federal authority to aid in the execution of federal law at Little Rock, Arkansas. This became necessary when my proclamation of yesterday was not observed, and the obstruction of justice still continues.

It is important that the reasons for my action be understood by all our citizens. As you know, the Supreme Court of the United States has decided that separate public educational facilities for the races are inherently unequal and therefore compulsory [forced] school segregation laws are unconstitutional.

Our personal opinions about the decision have no bearing on the matter of enforcement; the responsibility and authority of the Supreme Court to interpret the Constitution are very clear. Local federal courts were instructed by the Supreme Court to issue such orders and decrees as might be necessary to achieve admission to public schools without regard to race and with all deliberate [intentional] speed.

Source: National Archives

One of the most important tests took place in Little Rock, Arkansas in 1957. Nine African American students were registered to attend that city's Central High School. The governor of Arkansas, Orval Faubus, wanted to prevent them from entering the building. He called for the state's National Guard to help keep them out.

President Dwight D. Eisenhower had to uphold the law. He took command of the Arkansas National Guard and sent federal troops to protect the African American students.

The nine were able to attend school that year. The following year, the governor shut down the public schools and the state opened "private" academies. These private academies were closed to African Americans. It showed how far some people would go to keep segregation.

Malcolm X

Malcolm Little was born in Omaha, Nebraska in 1925. His family moved to Michigan after the Ku Klux Klan threatened his father. When Malcolm was six, his father died in an accident. Malcolm believed whites murdered him.

Kwanzaa

Maulan Ron Karenga (*kuh-REN-guh*) was a civil rights activist. He created a new African American holiday in 1966. This holiday is called Kwanzaa (*KWAN-zuh*), which is the Swahili word meaning "first fruits." The holiday is meant to remind African Americans to pass their values and cultural traditions on to the next generation. Kwanzaa begins on December 26 and lasts for seven days.

Malcolm dropped out of school in the eighth grade and turned to a life of crime. At age 21, Malcolm was sentenced to prison for burglary. In prison he studied the teachings of Elijah Muhammad. Muhammad was the leader of the **Nation of Islam** (see p. 61). Elijah Muhammad claimed that whites were devils and that African Americans should not live among them. As Malcolm became more deeply involved with the Nation of Islam, he adopted the "X" in place of his last name. It was a symbol of his stolen identity from the time when his ancestors were brought from Africa as slaves.

After his release from prison, Malcolm became a minister for the Nation of Islam. He ministered in New York City's Harlem. There, his message of self-defense for blacks and portrayal of whites as devils won praise from the African American community. As Malcolm's influence grew, Elijah Muhammad became jealous. In December 1963, Malcolm left the organization.

Malcolm travelled to Mecca, a holy place for Muslims, in Saudi Arabia. There, Malcolm met Muslims from the Middle East who preached equality of the races. It changed his outlook and when he returned to the United States, he changed his name to El-Hajj Malik El-Shabazz (*el-haj mal-EEK el-shuh-BAZ*). He

Malcolm X (Library of Congress)

still believed that racism was to blame for the lack of equality in the United States, but he stopped hating whites. He began urging blacks to identify with people of African heritage from around the world.

Malcolm preached unity and stressed the need for African Americans to take control of their own futures. In 1965, Malcolm used the slogan "ballots or bullets" to express his interest in having African Americans win political power. He warned listeners that a revolution was necessary to change U.S. society.

Malcolm soon became concerned that there was a plot to kill him. He believed that members of the Nation of Islam wanted him dead because he had rejected the separation of black and white societies. On February 21, 1965, Malcolm X was addressing a crowd in Harlem. Three men shot him. He died instantly at age 39. His death revealed the deep divisions in the African American Muslim community.

The goal of the March on Washington in 1963 was to pressure the government into passing a civil rights bill. In this photograph, taken during the march, Dr. Martin Luther King, Jr. can be seen in the front row, second from the left. (Library of Congress)

March on Washington Movement

The March on Washington refers to the demonstration that took place on August 28, 1963. A. Philip Randolph, who had threatened to march on Washington in 1941 to protest segregation in factories organized the march with Bayard Rustin, and other leaders. Protesters hoped to pressure Congress into passing a civil rights bill. A quarter of a million people gathered on the Mall in Washington, D.C., listening to speakers on the steps of the Lincoln Memorial. Of all the speeches, **Martin Luther King, Jr.**'s (see p. 84) "I Have a Dream" was best remembered.

Marshall, Thurgood

Thurgood Marshall was born in 1908 in Baltimore and earned his law degree from Howard University. He practiced law

Free At Last

On August 28, 1963, Martin Luther King, Jr., delivered a speech on the steps of the Lincoln Memorial in Washington, DC. Before a crowd of thousands, he described a future in which all people would be free.

When we let freedom ring, when we let it ring from every village and hamlet, we will be able to speed up that day when all of God's children will be able to join hands and sing in the words of that old Negro spiritual: "Free at last! Free at last! Thank God Almighty, we are free at last!"

Source: Martin Luther King, Jr., "I Have a Dream."

Thurgood Marshall (Library of Congress)

under Charles H. Houston, legal director for the **National Association for the Advancement of Colored People (NAACP)** (see p. 62). Marshall was a genius at using the law to challenge segregation and racism. Before working on the *Brown v. Board of Education* (see p. 81) case in 1954, Marshall worked on *McLaurin* v. *Oklahoma State* (1950) and *Sweatt* v. *Painter* (1950). In these two cases, Marshall argued successfully that African Americans had the right to study at "white" universities. In 1967, Marshall became the first African American to be appointed to the U.S. Supreme Court.

Montgomery Bus Boycott

Rosa Parks was a 42-year-old African American seamstress. On December 1, 1955 she got on a bus in Montgomery, Alabama. She took a seat in the "colored" section of the bus. When the white section filled up, the driver asked Parks to stand up and give her seat to whites. The law said she had to give her seat to a white person. That evening, however, Parks refused. The bus driver called the police and Parks was arrested for violating the **Jim Crow Laws** (see p. 24) of the South.

Parks was not only a seamstress. She was active in the **National Association for the Advancement of Colored People (NAACP)** (see p. 62) and served as secretary of a local chapter. When word got around about how she had been treated, the African American community was outraged. Leaders and community members met at the Dexter Avenue Church to decide on a plan of action. This was the church of young **Martin Luther King, Jr.** (see p. 84). The Women's Political Council, an African American group run by Jo Ann Robinson, called for a boycott of the buses in Montgomery. The others agreed. African Americans spread the word and organized car pools and walked to work.

The bus company, which relied on African American riders, lost money. The city of Montgomery jailed protesters. King's house was bombed. The boycott and other events were covered on the national news.

The boycott lasted for 381 days. In late 1956, the Supreme Court found that segregation on buses is unconstitutional. When the bus company desegregated, Martin Luther King and other African Americans climbed on board with a great deal of satisfaction.

Robinson, Jackie

Born in 1919, in Pasadena, California, Jackie Robinson played football in college at the University of California, Los Angeles. He then played for a professional football team known as the Los Angeles Bulldogs. After serving in the army during World War II, Robinson switched to baseball. He began playing for the Kansas City Monarchs of the Negro Leagues.

In 1946, Branch Rickey, general manager of the Brooklyn Dodgers, a major league baseball team, decided to sign Robinson as the first African American to play in the major leagues since the late 1800s. After playing for a Dodgers minor league team, Robinson was called up to Brooklyn in 1947. Despite verbal abuse and threats of violence from fellow players and fans, Robinson went on to win the respect of millions—both black and white. His lifetime batting average was .311, and he won the National League's Most Valuable Player award in 1949. He retired in 1956 and was elected to the Baseball Hall of Fame in 1962.

Sit-ins

Sit-ins were a nonviolent form of protest used by students to desegregate lunch counters. Throughout the South, **Jim Crow laws** (see p. 24) had separate seating for African American customers at lunch counters. In February 1960, four African American students in Greensboro, North Carolina, sat at the "whites only" lunch counter and asked to be served. They were refused service, but they sat all day. At the end of the day they left. The following day 20 students came to the lunch counter to "sit-in." On the third day some white students joined them.

The students would sit and wait to be served, refusing to move even in the face of verbal and physical abuse. African American students were beaten and arrested at the counters. As soon as one group was arrested, another group took their places. The sit-ins received national news coverage and proved embarrassing for the South. In Atlanta city officials made a deal with the students. Students would stop the sit-ins and jailed protesters would be released.

Many of the students who participated in the sit-ins formed the **Student Nonviolent Coordinating Committee (SNCC)** (see p. 93).

Southern Christian Leadership Conference (SCLC)

The Southern Christian Leadership Conference was made up of African American ministers from ten southern states. It was founded in 1957. **Martin Luther King, Jr.** (see p. 84) was elected the group's president. The SCLC worked to desegregate public transportation, pub-

In 1968, the Southern Christian Leadership Conference launched the Poor People's Campaign to bring attention to poverty among African Americans and other minorities (Private Collection)

lic schools, and all public places. They staged nonviolent protests to call for new legislation. In 1968, the SCLC planned to begin a campaign called the Poor People's Campaign. The campaign, intended to be the first large, multiracial movement, was meant to protest poverty among all poor people, not only African Americans. Just weeks before the campaign was to begin, Dr. Martin Luther King, Jr., was assassinated. After King's death, the SCLC continued under the leadership of Ralph Abernathy. Since 1998, the group has been led by Martin Luther King III, one of the sons of Dr. King.

sports, African Americans in

After World War II, sports became more integrated. In 1947, **Jackie Robinson** (see p. 91) joined the Brooklyn Dodgers as the first African American in organized professional baseball. In the years that followed, more blacks joined professional baseball teams.

During the 1960s, certain African American athletes became famous. Muhammad Ali was a heavyweight boxer who had won the world championship. He had to give the title up when he refused to serve in the army. He was protesting the Vietnam War.

In 1968, tennis star Arthur Ashe became the first African American to win the U.S. Open men's singles championship. In December 1968, O.J. Simpson, a running back for the University of Southern California, won the Heisman Trophy. That same year, at the Olympics in Mexico City, Tommie Smith and John Carlos won gold and silver medals in track and field. During the ceremonies they gave the **Black Power** (see p. 80) salute—a closed fist raised high overhead—to protest racism in the United States. They were suspended from the team.

Student Nonviolent Coordinating Committee (SNCC)

The Student Nonviolent Coordinating Committee was established in 1960. Its purpose was to organize and coordinate student protests. SNCC (pronounced "snick") wanted to integrate public lunch counters, rest rooms, parks, theaters, and schools. They also registered African American voters.

Stokely Carmichael, one of the leaders of SNCC and the Black Power movement. (Library of Congress)

SNCC was a major force during the civil rights movement. SNCC members took part in the **Freedom Rides** (see p. 82), the **March on Washington** (see p. 89), and other major events. For the summer of 1964, SNCC organized a huge campaign in Mississippi with three goals: registering voters, operating Freedom Schools, and organizing the Mississippi Freedom Democratic Party (MFDP) precincts. That summer became known as **Freedom Summer** (see p. 83).

The Freedom Schools gave rural children a chance to get an education. Registering voters was dangerous. White southerners killed several SNCC members and African Americans who had dared to register. Local laws had excluded blacks from the

Democratic Party. The MFDP was an attempt to have a Democratic Party that included African Americans. The MFDP went to the Democratic National Convention in 1964. It tried to prove it was the party that truly represented Mississippi. Lyndon Johnson, the presidential nominee, refused to seat the MFDP. He did not want to push away white southern voters.

In 1966, Stokely Carmichael headed SNCC and the organization adopted his **Black Power** (see p. 80) philosophy. Carmichael discouraged SNCC from recruiting whites. He said that African Americans needed to develop their own culture, not to become part of white society. Carmichael made an alliance with the **Black Panther Party** (see p. 79) for a time, but eventually broke away from them as well.

Voting Rights Act of 1965

In January 1965, the civil rights movement was waging a fight for its life in the South. **Martin Luther King, Jr.** (see p. 84), and the **Southern Christian Leadership Council (SCLC)** (see p. 92) had been working hard to make the nation aware of the plight of African American voters in the Deep South. African Americans were often not allowed to register. If they did register, they were kept from voting. Southerners used threats, beatings, and lynchings to scare African Americans away. When **Student Nonviolent Coordinating Committee (SNCC)** (see p. 93) volunteers arrived in Alabama to register people to vote, the police began throwing African Americans in jail.

King hoped to expose the violence to the public. He staged a 50-mile march from Selma to Montgomery, the capital of Alabama. Once at the capital, King would ask the governor to protect African American voters.

The march began on Sunday, March 7, 1965. Police officers in Selma attacked the marchers with tear gas and clubs. Television cameras documented the scene, which became known as "Bloody Sunday." Angered, people from around the country, sympathetic with the marchers, rushed to Selma to join the march. The following week President Lyndon B. Johnson announced his support for a voting rights bill. The bill would allow federal examiners to register African American voters where there was discrimination.

Mississippi Summer Project, 1964

The Student Nonviolent Coordinating Committee created a pamphlet that stated its mission for what would come to be called "Freedom Summer."

....**A**s the winds of change grow stronger, the threatened political elite of Mississippi becomes more **intransigent** and fanatical...Negro efforts to win the right to vote cannot succeed...without a nationwide mobilization of support. A program is planned for this summer which will involve the massive participation of Americans dedicated to the elimination of racial oppression...

Source: Library of Congress

◀ **intransigent**
uncompromising

On March 17, SCLC (see p. 92) and **SNCC** (see p. 93) received a permit from a federal judge to complete their march. Six days later, Martin Luther King, Jr., and Ralph Bunche led 25,000 marchers to Montgomery. Sometime later President Johnson signed the Voting Rights Act of 1965 into law.

Wallace, George

George Wallace served as governor of Alabama between 1963 and 1967, and again from 1971 to 1979 and 1983 to 1987. He became nationally known during his first campaign for governor, when he pledged "Segregation now and segregation forever!" The following year, he personally stood in the doorway of University of Alabama to block African American students from entering. As a result, the federal government sent the National Guard to desegregate the school. Wallace later campaigned unsuccessfully for president. In 1968, he ran as an independent candidate, winning five Southern states. In 1972, he competed to be the Democratic Party's nominee. His campaign ended when he was shot and paralyzed during a campaign stop.

CHAPTER FOUR

The Struggle Continues

The Late 20th Century, 1969–Present

"America is not like a blanket—one piece of unbroken cloth, the same color, the same texture, the same size. America is more like a quilt—many patches, many pieces, many colors, many sizes, all woven and held together by a common thread."

—The Reverend Jesse Jackson

In 1968, many Americans were tired of unrest. Robert F. Kennedy, brother of President John F. Kennedy, had been assassinated, just as his brother had five years before. Dr. Martin Luther King, Jr., the best-known leader of the African American civil rights movement, had also been killed, sparking riots in many cities. Police and protesters had also clashed violently during the summer in Chicago, where the Democratic Party had gathered to choose its presidential candidate. Finally, the Vietnam War continued to drag on, further dividing the nation.

Because of the events and unrest of 1968, there were demands for law and order from many Americans in 1969. The Democratic Party, which had become associated with much of the unrest, lost the White House. Republican Richard Nixon defeated former vice president Hubert Humphrey. Nixon promised to end the war in Vietnam and restore calm at home.

The war did not end, however. Nixon and his national security advisor, Henry Kissinger, continued the war until 1973. Large numbers of young black men served in Vietnam. In one year, 64 percent of eligible African

Americans were drafted, as opposed to 31 percent of eligible whites. In the end, 20 percent of all those killed and wounded were black. At that time, African Americans made up only 9.3 percent of the U.S. population.

NEW OPPORTUNITIES FOR AFRICAN AMERICANS

Back home in the United States, Nixon put an end to the anti-poverty programs that had taken place under the president before him, Lyndon Johnson. However, he did address some African American concerns. He set goals for the hiring of minorities on federal construction projects. He also pressed colleges to increase their numbers of minority students and faculty. In 1972, Congress passed the **Equal Employment Opportunity Act** (see p. 110). This allowed companies and other organizations to be sued for gender discrimination.

The efforts of the civil rights movement of the 1960s began to pay off in the 1970s. Barriers began to tumble. In 1971, Samuel Gravely became the first African American admiral in the U.S. Navy. In 1973, three cities elected African American mayors: Atlanta (Maynard Jackson), Detroit (Coleman Young) and Los Angeles (Tom Bradley) (see **politics, African Americans in**, p. 118). In 1974, Frank Robinson became the first African American to manage a major league baseball team. As more barriers were crossed, the movement focused on creating opportunities for a larger number of people.

Timeline

1972

Shirley Chisolm becomes the first African American to run for president of the United States, when she seeks the Democratic Party's nomination for the presidency.

1973

Maynard Jackson becomes mayor of Atlanta, Georgia.

AFFIRMATIVE ACTION AND SCHOOL DESEGREGATION

Meanwhile, some people complained that efforts to provide opportunities for African Americans were unfair to whites. In 1978, the U.S. Supreme Court struck down the **affirmative action** (see p. 105) policy of the University of California. White medical school applicant Alan Bakke had been turned down. The court said this was done unfairly because of a system of racial quotas. However, the court said that race could still be a factor in admissions policies. The following year the court upheld a job-training program even though it created racial imbalance. In 1988, the **Civil Rights Restoration Act** (see p. 108) said that any institution receiving federal funds could not discriminate. Institutions often rejected federal funds so that they could continue to maintain programs as they saw fit.

Since the 1954 Supreme Court decision of *Brown v. Board of Education* (see p. 81), school segregation had been illegal. But as late as the 1970s, many schools resisted integration. Often, the argument against integration was that children went to school in their own neighborhoods. The neighborhoods themselves were segregated. Some school districts began to bus students outside their neighborhoods to integrate schools. In 1971, the Supreme Court ruled in *Swann* v. *Charlotte-Mecklenburg Board of Education* (in North Carolina). They said it was legal to bus students for this purpose. Two years later, in *Keys* v. *School District #1, Denver* (Colorado), the court struck down a **busing** plan (see p. 107) to carry African American

1975	1976	1978	1979
Frank Robinson becomes the first African American to manage a major league baseball team.	Barbara Jordan becomes the first African American woman to deliver the keynote address at the Democratic Party's presidential convention.	The U.S. Supreme Court rules that the University of California has practiced "reverse discrimination" by denying admission to white applicant Alan Bakke.	Executive Robert L. Johnson founds Black Entertainment Television (BET), the nation's first and only African American–owned cable station.

students from their neighborhood schools to those in mostly white neighborhoods. Many white students were bused to schools in black neighborhoods.

After the death of **Martin Luther King, Jr.** (see p. 84), no single African American civil rights leader held the respect of the large majority. Although many African American civil rights leaders enjoyed the support of Democrat President Jimmy Carter (1977-1981), by the end of the 1970s the nation had become more conservative. In 1980, Republican Ronald Reagan took office. He, like many conservatives, opposed laws that in his view, gave too much authority to the federal government. He also feared that programs like affirmative action discriminated against whites. Reagan also felt that federal taxes were too high. After Congress passed a large cut in taxes, Reagan began to cut spending for anti-poverty programs, such as housing assistance and nutrition programs for poor children.

JESSE JACKSON

Because many of the poor were African Americans, civil rights leaders feared that the gains of the 1960s and 1970s were being lost. Many of these concerns were voiced by **Jesse Jackson** (see p. 114), who ran for president in 1984, and again in 1988.

Jackson was an associate of Martin Luther King, Jr. In 1971, Jackson had founded People United to Save Humanity (PUSH). PUSH worked to stop

1983	**1984**	**1985**	**1988**
Julius "Dr. J" Irving leads the Philadelphia 76ers to the NBA title.	Jesse Jackson makes his first run for president.	Oprah Winfrey begins hosting her own nationally syndicated talk show, *The Oprah Winfrey Show*.	Author Toni Morrison wins the Pulitzer Prize for her novel, *Beloved*.

drugs, teenage pregnancy and violence. This gave Jackson a platform on which to run. He organized the Rainbow Coalition. It was made up of various racial and ethnic groups. In 1984, Jackson won Democratic primaries in nine states and received 7 million votes. By 1988, when Jackson again ran for the nomination he had become a household name. Although he failed to win the Democratic nomination in either attempt, he brought issues of importance to many African Americans to the public's attention. From then on, Jackson was a national figure. He became involved in various international events. When Bill Clinton became president in 1992, Jackson became an unofficial advisor.

Louis Farrakhan and the Million Man March

While many of the 1960s civil rights figures were Christian, Islam kept a strong foothold in the African American community. The religion could trace its roots to the days of slavery. About 10 percent of those brought from Africa were Muslim. The American Muslim movement began in the 1930s when Elijah Muhammad began the **Nation of Islam** (see p. 61) in Chicago. After his death in 1975, his son founded the American Muslim Mission. By the 1990s, there were more than 5 million Muslims in the United States. The Nation of Islam had become only a small part of a larger movement.

Louis Farrakhan is one of the most controversial figures in the Nation of Islam. At first he was known for his hate speech regarding Jews and a pos-

1988	1989	1991	1992
Temple University becomes the first to offer a Ph.D. program in **African American studies**.	Filmmaker Spike Lee releases his controversial film, *Do the Right Thing*.	**Clarence Thomas** is appointed to the U.S. Supreme Court, becoming the second African American to serve on the court in history.	The second worst riots in American history, after the Civil War draft riots, erupt in Los Angeles after police filmed beating motorist Rodney King are acquitted of any crime.

sible connection to the death of **Malcolm X** (see p. 87). In 1995 he gained new respect as one of the organizers of the **Million Man March** (see p. 117). This was one of the largest demonstrations ever held in Washington. The marchers apologized for past irresponsible behavior and said they were ready to take responsibility for the African American family. The all-male event was criticized by Farrakhan's opponents and by African American women who felt excluded. The event was generally considered positive. Filmmaker Spike Lee (see **television and movies, African Americans in**, p. 122) even made a film about it, *Get On the Bus*.

Hate Crimes and the L.A. Riots

Between 1882 and 1961, 3,442 African Americans had been lynched. Now lynching was replaced by what came to be called **hate crimes** (see p. 111). Crimes based on race, religion, or national origin were made federal offenses in 1968. In 1995, there were 2,988 reported hate crimes directed against African Americans. These ranged from cross-burnings to murder.

For many African Americans, the criminal justice system seemed against people of color. There were incidents of racial profiling. This meant police targeted non-whites for searches and questioning. There were police brutality charges against white police who beat black suspects. One such case is that of Rodney King. He is a black man who was beaten by police after a car chase in Los Angeles in 1991. This led to days of riots (see **Los Angeles**

1992	1993	1993	1994
Carol Mosely Braun becomes the first African American woman elected to the U.S. Senate.	Michael Jordan leads the Chicago Bulls to their third consecutive NBA title.	The Chicago Bears' Walter Payton is inducted into the Football Hall of Fame.	Nelson Mandela is elected president of South Africa in the first multi-racial election in South African history.

riots, p. 116). There were mistaken shootings of African Americans such as Amadou Diallo (*AHM-uh-doo dee-AHL-oo*). Diallo was an African immigrant in New York. Police thought he was reaching for a gun when he was reaching for his wallet. They fired 41 bullets, killing him. They were tried and acquitted of any wrongdoing in this incident.

CLARENCE THOMAS

Within the black community there were also divisions over the state of race relations. A majority of African American intellectuals favored affirmative action and other programs to address what they saw as ongoing injustices. However, a small number of conservative blacks opposed them. This divide had become apparent in 1991 when President George Bush nominated **Clarence Thomas** (see p. 124), an African American, to become the second African American Supreme Court justice, after **Thurgood Marshall** (see p. 89). Because he opposed affirmative action and giving welfare benefits to single mothers, most civil rights groups did not support Thomas. The Senate confirmed Thomas, however, and he joined the court.

ACHIEVEMENTS IN BUSINESS AND ARTS

Although the last 30 years have been a time of great change for African Americans, they have also been a time of great achievement for African Americans in all walks of life. Over the last three decades, great writers

1995	**1996**	**1999**	**2000**
Controversial Nation of Islam leader Louis Farrakhan leads the **Million Man March** in Washington.	President Bill Clinton signs the Church Arson Prevention Act.	New York City police shoot and kill Guinean immigrant Amadou Diallo.	Tennis star Venus Williams wins the women's singles title at Wimbledon.

(see **literature, African Americans in**, p. 115) such as Toni Morrison, Alex Haley, and Alice Walker have helped millions of readers of all races better understand the experiences of African Americans. Artists from jazz great Miles Davis to rapper Tupac Shakur (see **music, African Americans in**, p. 117) have broken new ground in expressing themselves through music. Athletes like Michael Jordan, Venus and Serena Williams, and Tiger Woods have soared to new heights (see **sports, African Americans in**, p. 120). On television and in the movies, stars like Bill Cosby, Oprah Winfrey, and Denzel Washington have entertained and educated Americans of all races (see **television and film, African Americans in**, p. 122).

Although many African Americans still face obstacles, the African American community continues to make great strides. Community leaders, such as **Clara McBride Hale** (see p. 110), founder of Hale House, is one example of a leader who helped many of those still struggling. In the business world, many African American business people (see **business, African Americans in**, p. 106) are dedicating themselves to teaching young people how to prepare for success. As African American history moves into the 21st century, the community's long history of overcoming great obstacles and injustices will surely continue for generations.

2001 2001

Kenneth Chenault becomes the first African American Chief Executive Officer (CEO) of a Fortune-500 company when he is named CEO of American Express.

President George W. Bush appoints **Colin Powell** secretary of state. Powell will play a major role in the War on Terrorism and the War in Iraq.

A-Z of Key People, Events, and Terms

African American studies

In the late 1960s, African Americans wanted African American history and culture courses to be taught in colleges. Beginning in the 1970s, many colleges and universities did begin to offer these courses. In 1988, Temple University became the first to offer a Ph.D. program in African American studies. By the year 2000, there were at least 200 colleges offering B.A.-level degree programs in African American studies, and eight offering graduate degrees. Several African American Studies professors, including Cornel West of Princeton University in Princeton, New Jersey and Henry Louis Gates of Harvard University in Cambridge, Massachusetts, have become nationally known.

affirmative action

During the 1970s, federal, state, and city governments started "affirmative action" programs. These were aimed at helping minorities get fair treatment in business and education. Many of these programs have led to policies that have included quotas. These quotas require a certain percentage of minorities to be hired or admitted to colleges. Some people believe these "affirmative action" policies are unfair to whites. In 1978, the Supreme Court ruled on affirmative action in the case of *Bakke* v. *University of California*. Alan Bakke was a white male. He applied for admission to the University of California's medical school. The court ruled that he had been denied admission in favor of a less qualified African American. The court said this was "reverse discrimination." They called for stricter guidelines in future cases.

Some states have passed laws ending affirmative action. In 1996, California ended quotas in its public universities. This caused a decrease in the number of African Americans admitted.

In more recent years, critics of affirmative action have worked to make using race as a factor in hiring or in admitting students to a school illegal. In 2003, the administration of

President George W. Bush challenged the University of Michigan's right to use race as one factor in deciding which students to admit.

apartheid

Apartheid is racial segregation or "separate development." It was introduced by the white government of South Africa in 1948. This was a way to strengthen white domination over the nation. Over the next 40 years thousands of protesters were jailed or killed. The African National Congress party opposed apartheid. In 1960 this party was outlawed. In 1964, Nelson Mandela, an ANC leader, was jailed for life. After this international opposition to apartheid grew. This caused governments and investors around the world to stop doing business with South Africa. In 1990, at age 72, Nelson Mandela was freed. This began the end of the apartheid system. In 1994, Mandela was elected president of South Africa. This was the first election in which black South Africans were allowed to vote.

business, African Americans in

During the late 20th century, African Americans made many gains in business. Today, several of the most powerful companies in the United States are headed by African Americans. Among these leaders are Stanley O'Neal of the financial services company Merrill Lynch; Ken Chenault, who heads American Express, another financial services company; Richard Parsons, the top executive of media and Internet giant AOL Time Warner; and Franklin Raines, CEO of Fannie Mae, a company that finances home mortgages. Oprah Winfrey, the television talk show host, and head of Harpo, Inc., her production company, is America's most successful businesswoman, and also the first African American billionaire.

Despite these success stories, African Americans still fall behind the population in general when it comes to reaching the top levels of business success. African Americans make up about 10 percent of the American population. However, as of 2002, only five—or one percent—of Fortune-500 companies (an annual list of the most valuable companies published by *Fortune* magazine) are led by African Americans. Many African

Americans never rise beyond the lower and middle levels of corporations.

According to some experts, one reason may be that African
Americans do not have the same number of mentors, or experi-
enced informal advisors as white professionals. However, organizations such as Executive Leadership Council (ELC) in
Washington, D.C., which is made up of 264 senior African
American executives in Fortune-500 companies are examples of
groups that aim to create strong networks for African American
professionals of the future.

busing

Even though they were illegal, segregated schools continued to
exist for many years. In the South, many school officials refused
to enforce anti-segregation laws. Also, many white families left the
cities. So, many city schools were made up of mostly African
American and other minority students. Local governments and the
federal courts wanted to make sure all students received a quality
education. In the 1970s, the Supreme Court allowed the use of
busing. This meant whites were bused to schools in mostly African

Police lead African American children off a bus into school in Boston during the the 1970s. (Library of Congress)

American neighborhoods, while African Americans were bused to white neighborhoods. This led to protests and even acts of violence, mostly by white parents.

Starting in 1976, a new method of trying to desegregate large city public schools has been attempted. The goal of magnet schools is to create schools that attract white students to inner-city schools where most students are African American or from another minority group. To attract white students, magnet schools emphasize special courses, such as performing arts, math, science or technology. By attracting white students to these schools, the goal is to make each school more racially balanced.

Some people have criticized the magnet school idea. These critics say that in order to achieve racial balance, many of these magnet schools have turned away African American students in order to admit whites. However, by the end of the 1990s, magnet schools had replaced busing as a way to desegregate many school systems. During the 1999-2000 school year, school systems across the nation operated 1,372 magnet schools, according to the National Center for Education Statistics.

Civil Rights Restoration Act

In 1984, the U.S. Supreme Court decision in the case *Grove City* v. *Bell* limited how the landmark Civil Rights Act of 1964 could be used to defend against discrimination. In the case, a small Pennsylvania college argued that it should still be entitled to federal funds, even if it did not offer as many school sports opportunities to women, since the federal money the school received was not used in the sports program. In 1987, however, the U.S. Congress repealed the Supreme Court's decision. It passed the Civil Rights Restoration Act of 1987. The law stated that no recipient of federal funds could legally discriminate in any of its programs or activities, even if the money was not directly used in that program. Although *Grove City* v. *Bell* was specifically about women's sports, the Supreme Court's decision, and the Civil Rights Restoration Act affected racial discrimination as well.

education

Throughout much of American history, African Americans have been denied the opportunity for quality education that many

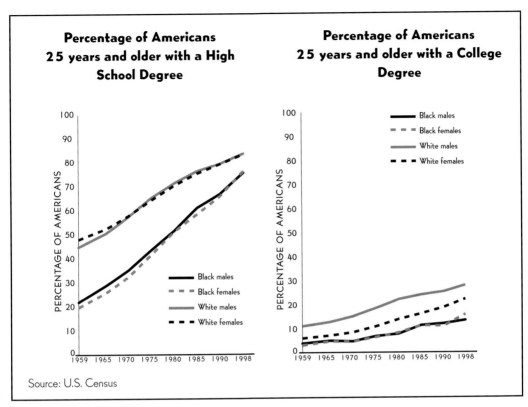

Percentage of Americans 25 years and older with a High School Degree

Percentage of Americans 25 years and older with a College Degree

Source: U.S. Census

other Americans have enjoyed. In fact, many of the greatest civil rights battles have been over the right of African Americans to receive quality educations. Since the landmark 1954 *Brown* v. *Board of Education* ruling by the Supreme Court, it has been illegal to maintain separate schools for black and white students. In that case, the Supreme Court overruled the 1896 *Plessy* v. *Ferguson* decision that stated that public facilities that are "separate but equal" are legal.

Despite the ruling, however, many African Americans continued to attend schools where there were very few white students. This has happened because many city neighborhoods are mostly black or from another minority group and therefore and therefore most of the students attending these schools are also minorities. It has also happened because since the 1970s many middle class and wealthy whites have left the cities to move to suburbs. In general, suburban public schools have provided better educations than public schools in cities since local suburban governments have more money to improve them.

Since the 1970s, efforts have been made to desegregate, or

balance, the racial make-up of schools. Methods like mandatory **busing** (see p. 107) and the creation of magnet schools have been used to achieve this goal.

Although African Americans have continued to lag behind white Americans in educational achievement, the gap has closed in recent years. In 1980, only 51 percent of African Americans over the age of 25 had completed high school, versus 69 percent for the population as a whole. By 1999, 77 percent of African Americans over age 25 had completed high school, versus 83 percent of all Americans.

College enrollment has also increased. Just 8 percent of all African Americans over age 25 had earned college diplomas by 1980. By 1999, the figure had doubled to 16 percent.

Equal Employment Opportunity Act

This federal law was passed by Congress in 1972. It promoted equal job opportunities for all Americans. It also established the Equal Employment Opportunity Commission (EEOC). The law made it illegal for an employer to fail or refuse to hire a job applicant because of his or her sex. The law also made it illegal to pay workers different salaries for the same job based only on whether they are male or female. This law helped many African American women find new opportunities in the workplace that had previously been denied.

Clara McBride Hale (Hale House)

Hale, Clara McBride

President Ronald Reagan called Clara McBride Hale a "true American hero." "Mother" Hale took in homeless and sick babies and cared for them. Some of these children had been born addicted to drugs such as heroin or crack cocaine, while others were born with the HIV virus that causes *AIDS*, a usually fatal disease. She did this in her home beginning in 1941. By the mid-1970s, Mother Hale turned her apartment into a licensed childcare center.

Hale House has cared for more than 800 infants from Harlem neighborhoods. Following "Mother" Hale's death in 1992, Hale House was led by her daughter, Lorraine Hale. During the 1990s, Hale House grew in the number of services it provided. However, in 2001, Lorraine Hale stepped down from her job after she pleaded guilty to stealing Hale House money. Since then, Hale House has continued its work under new leadership.

hate crimes

Since the end of the civil rights movement of the 1960s, crimes committed because of the race of the victim or victims have become less common. Many of the people who participated in famous crimes against African Americans have finally been sent to jail. However, organizations and individuals who commit crimes based on racial hatred have continued to commit acts of violence against African Americans and other minorities. According to the Southern Poverty Law Center, a group that tracks these crimes, as of 2000, there were still as many as 138 branches of the Ku Klux Klan. There are also many other groups, such as neo-Nazis, (modern-day followers of Adolf Hitler) who have also committed crimes against African Americans. Some of

A Ku Klux Klan rally in suburban Maryland in 1980. (Library of Congress)

these groups started during the 1990s. Often they have used the Internet to attract new members. In 1995, there was only one "hate group" site on the Internet. Five years later, there were 2,000. Many of these hate groups have argued that the United States should be a "white man's country."

Both local and federal law enforcement officials have made a special effort in recent years to combat groups like the Klan. In 1995 and 1996, more than 200 African American churches throughout the South were burned, some by members of the Klan. In response, President Bill Clinton signed the Church Arson Prevention Act, providing financial loans to help rebuild those churches. Many states and cities have passed "Hate Crimes" laws that make the penalties for those committing crimes based on race even stricter. Critics of these laws have argued that these laws are unnecessary and that stricter enforcement of existing laws is a better alternative.

health, African Americans and

Health is another area in which African Americans fall behind white Americans. According to recent studies, a black male child born in the year 2000 is likely to live 64.6 years, while a white male can expect to live until age 73. For females, the gap is not as large. Black females born in the year 2000 can expect to live to be nearly 75, while white females will live to be about 80.

Average life expectancy, or length of life, is just one health area where African Americans fall behind whites. For example, infant mortality rates, or the percentage of babies that die before age one, was almost three times as high among African Americans as for whites.

African Americans also tend to suffer from various health problems more often than whites. Blacks had a rate of death from heart disease 50 percent higher than whites. Blacks are nearly twice as likely to die from stroke.

Experts believe that many of these higher health risks are caused by greater poverty among African Americans. Poverty is also one reason that far more blacks die from violence than is the case with whites. According to studies in the late 1990s, blacks were nearly seven times more likely to be murdered than whites.

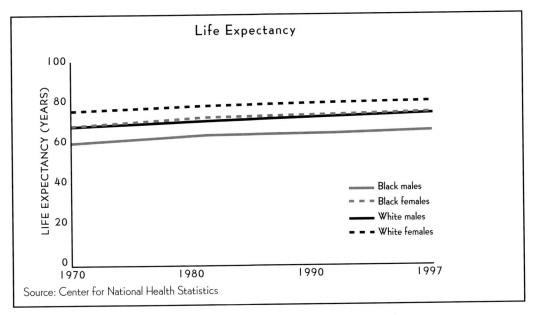

Life Expectancy

Source: Center for National Health Statistics

While less than 17 percent of white children under the age of 18 lived in poverty, the rate for black youths was nearly 44 percent in the mid-1990s.

Lack of health insurance is another major reason for poorer health on average among African Americans. White children were far less likely to be without health insurance than black children. In addition, African Americans were less likely to have visited a doctor's office over the course of a year than whites. At the same time, they were far more likely to see a doctor in a hospital. Experts believe this is because African Americans who cannot afford regular visits to the doctor wait until their illnesses become more serious to be treated.

Some critics also believe that prejudice may play a role in health differences between African Americans and whites. According to a 1999 survey of 720 physicians conducted by the National Heart, Lung, and Blood Institute, doctors were less likely to order a procedure called cardiac (heart) catheterization (*cath-et-ur-ih-ZAY-shun*) for black patients complaining of chest pains than for whites. Catheterization is considered the best diagnostic procedure for determining heart problems.

Immigration, African and Caribbean
Most of the early Africans to come to America came against their will, as slaves. Even during the 20th century, most emigrants from

Jesse Jackson (Rainbow Coalition)

Africa went to Europe. Voluntary immigration from Africa to the United States increased after the passage of a less strict immigration law in 1965. This also resulted in a much higher number of immigrants of African descent from the Caribbean, Guyana and Belize. These people have come for economic or educational reasons. Many also arrive as refugees from political oppression or wars, such as violence in Haiti. Like other immigrants, many of these new Americans have settled in larger cities.

Jackson, Jesse

Born in Greenville, South Carolina in 1941, Jesse Louis Jackson is a well-known leader in the African American community. After attending North Carolina Agricultural and Technical University and Chicago Theological Seminary, Jackson became an assistant to Reverend **Martin Luther King, Jr.** (see p. 84). With King's support, Jackson founded Operation Breadbasket in Chicago in 1966. The goal of the program was to expand education and job opportunities for African Americans in Chicago. In 1971, Jackson left the **Southern Christian Leadership Conference** (see p. 92) and started People United to Save Humanity (PUSH). Jackson served as PUSH's president until 1983. In 1984, he made his first run for president. He ran a second time in 1988. Throughout the 1980s and 1990s, Jackson was involved in international events, from hostage negotiation to serving as emissary to South Africa. He is president of the Rainbow Coalition. Jackson began this organization to continue the fight for the rights of minorities in the U.S.

literature, African Americans in

During the last quarter of the 20th century, many African American novelists, poets, and other writers gained national attention. One of the best-known is Toni Morrison, author of such novels as *The Bluest Eye* (1970), *Song of Solomon* (1977), which became the first book published by an African American to be selected by the Book-of-the-Month Club since 1940, and *Beloved* (1990), which won the Pulitzer Prize.

Novelist, short-story writer and poet Alice Walker frequently writes about the efforts of African American women to find their own identities in a world dominated by whites and black men. Her first book, a collection of poetry entitled *Once*, was published in 1968. Her best-known work, *The Color Purple*, was awarded the Pulitzer Prize in 1982, and made into a film directed by Steven Spielberg, starring Whoopi Goldberg and Oprah Winfrey.

Best known for her poetry, Maya Angelou is also a historian, songwriter, playwright, dancer, stage and screen producer, director, performer, singer, and civil rights activist. Her autobiography *I Know Why the Caged Bird Sings* (1969) was nominated for the National Book Award. Among her books of poetry are: *A Brave and Startling Truth* (1995), *Wouldn't Take Nothing for My Journey Now* (1993), and *Just Give Me a Cool Drink of Water 'fore I Die*

Toni Morrison (Library of Congress)

(1971), which was nominated for the Pulitzer Prize. In 1993, Angelou wrote and delivered a poem, "On The Pulse of the Morning," at the inauguration for President Bill Clinton.

One of the best-known works of the late 20th century by an African American author is *Roots*, by Alex Haley. The book, which traces Haley's ancestors both in the United States and in Africa, was made into a 12-hour television miniseries that aired in 1977. The television program was watched by 130 million Americans when it appeared in 1977, making it the one of the most watched television series of all time. The show also inspired millions of African Americans to pursue an interest in genealogy.

Los Angeles riots

On March 3, 1991, Rodney King, an African American motorist, was pulled over and beaten by Los Angeles police. The event was captured on videotape by a passer-by. Shown on newscasts across the U.S. and the world, the videotape symbolized police abuse for many African Americans. When the police officers involved were found innocent in April 1992, riots erupted in South Central Los Angeles and spread to other areas in the city. For three days, Los Angeles was gripped by violence and looting. It was the worst riot in American history since the New York Draft Riots (see **race riots**, Vol. 1, p. 122) during the **Civil War** (see Vol. 1, p. 108).

Alex Haley's book *Roots*, which traced his family back through slavery to Africa, was made into a television miniseries. Actor Lavar Burton is seen here in his role as Kunta Kinte, after the character's capture in Africa. (*Movie Star News*)

Million Man March

The Million Man March, officially known as A Day of Atonement, took place on October 16, 1995. The event was organized by Benjamin Chavis of the **National Association for the Advancement of Colored People (NAACP)** (see p. 62), and featured a speech by controversial **Nation of Islam** (see p. 61) leader Louis Farrakhan. On that day, over 900,000 African American men gathered on the Washington, D.C. mall to promise to take responsibility for themselves, their families, African American women, the African American community, and the nation as a whole. Popularly known as the Million Man March, the October 16, 1995 event brought some 900,000 black men to Washington. Most Americans viewed the march positively, although many African American women were critical because women organizers excluded them. Three years later, a smaller Million Woman March was organized in Philadelphia.

music, African Americans in

During the last several decades of the 20th century, music by African Americans continued to have a great influence on American culture. During the 1970s, older forms of music, such as **jazz** (see p. 58) found new audiences, as legends like Miles Davis found ways to mix traditional jazz with rock and roll in a new jazz style known as fusion. At the same time, African American rock musicians, such as Jimi Hendrix, began using jazz styles in their rock and roll. Meanwhile, in the 1980s and 1990s, younger jazz artists, such as Wynton Marsalis, helped teach audiences about the older, more traditional forms of jazz, while also recording classical music as well.

Even more popular were African American music styles known as soul and rhythm and blues (R&B). Artists such as Aretha Franklin, Stevie Wonder, and Marvin Gaye sold millions of records during the 1970s and 1980s. In more recent years, these legends have been joined by artists such as TLC, Mariah Carey, and Toni Braxton.

One new style of black music that has changed the shape of popular music is known as rap. Rap songs usually are made up of a vocalist, or "rapper" who uses spoken words over a musical background. Often the music is electronic drum beats mixed with samples (short sound bites) from other songs. Rap music was first heard in the Bronx section of New York City in the late 1970s. Some of the first "rappers" were children of immigrants from Jamaica, where a similar style of music known as "dancehall" was popular.

Although early rap artists such as Grandmaster Flash, the Sugar Hill Gang, and Afrika Bambaataa (*Bomb-BAHT-uh*) had local followings, it was not until the mid-1980s when a group from Queens, New York called Run-DMC recorded a rap version of a song by the white rock band Aerosmith, that rap music gained the attention of both black and white audiences in both cities and suburbs.

During the late 1980s and early 1990s, many rap artists began to include political messages in their music. The Brooklyn, New York–based Public Enemy wrote songs about racism and violence by police against African Americans. The Los Angeles group N.W.A. and the Oakland, California rapper Tupac Shakur wrote songs that were often about the violence of life in African American ghettos. Although many criticized these groups for their controversial lyrics, defenders said they were simply trying to show life as it was for them.

During the 1990s, rap continued to influence popular music. In time, it also helped change the way teenagers and other young people spoke and dressed. As the 21st century began, rap's influence showed no signs of weakening.

politics, African Americans in

With passage of the Voting Rights Act of 1965, millions of African Americans in the southern U.S. were able to vote for the first time. The law had a major impact, as African Americans were soon being elected to local, state, and national offices in their largest numbers since **Reconstruction** (See Vol. I, p. 123).

For example, in 1973, Maynard Jackson became the first African American mayor of a southeastern city when he was elected major of Atlanta, Georgia in 1973. Another is Andrew Young, who, as executive vice president of the **Southern Christian Leadership Conference** (see p. 92) helped to write and convince the U.S. Congress to pass the **1964 Civil Rights Act** (see p. 82). In 1973, he became the first black to serve as a

Andrew Young (Library of Congress)

member of the U.S. House of Representatives from Georgia since the 1870s. In 1977, President Jimmy Carter selected Young to serve as the U.S. Ambassador to the United Nations. During the 1980s, Young follow Maynard Jackson as mayor of Atlanta.

Women politicians have also made great strides winning office in the South. In 1966, Barbara Jordan became the first African American to serve in the Texas State Senate in 83 years. In 1972, she became the first African American elected to Congress since 1898. In 1976, she became the first African American— and first woman—to serve as keynote speaker at the Democratic National Convention.

Northern politicians also had great achievements in the late 20th century. Carl Stokes of Cleveland and Richard Hatcher of Gary, Indiana were both elected mayors of their cities in 1966. Shirley Chisolm of Brooklyn, New York became the first African American woman elected to the U.S. Congress in 1968. In 1972, she became the first African American woman to seek her party's nomination for president, and in 1984, she founded the National Political Caucus of Black Women.

Yet another ground-breaking African American woman is Carol Moseley-Braun of Illinois. In 1992, she became the first African American woman senator in history. Despite losing her reelection bid in 1998, Mosely-Braun announced in 2003 that she intended to run for president in 2004.

Muhammad Ali

Ali announces his conversion to Islam. He holds a book by Nation of Islam leader Elijah Muhammad. (Library of Congress)

Cassius Clay was born in Louisville, Kentucky in 1942. In 1962 he won a gold medal for boxing at the Olympics and soon after become a professional. When he knocked out heavyweight champion Sonny Liston in 1964, Clay became famous. The next day, he announced that he had converted to Islam and changed his name to Muhammad Ali. In 1967, he refused to be drafted for service in the Vietnam War. The reason he gave was that his religion forbade it. As a result, boxing officials took away his title from him. His stand against the war made him a hero to millions of young African Americans and others who opposed the war.

In 1971, Ali returned to the ring, but was defeated by Joe Frazier. In 1974, he regained the heavyweight champion title, though he lost it again in 1978.

Powell, Colin

Colin Powell was born in New York City's Harlem in 1937. He was raised in the Bronx by his Jamaican immigrant parents. After graduating from City College of New York in 1958, he enrolled in infantry school as a lieutenant. He served two tours in Vietnam, and then served as military aide to top civilian officials in the Pentagon. During the 1980s, he became President Ronald Reagan's National Security Adviser. By 1988, he had become a four-star general, and the following year he was promoted to become the Chairman of the Joint Chiefs of Staff, the highest-ranking military officer, other than the president. In 1991, General Powell became the first African American to lead a U.S. war, when the United States sent troops into the Persian Gulf region to turn back Iraq's invasion of Kuwait. In 2001, he was chosen to serve as Secretary of State by President George W. Bush. In that role, he has helped to devise strategy in the U.S. War on Terrorism. Prior to the Iraq War, he also played a prominent, though unsuccessful part in attempting to win United Nations Security Council support for that war.

sports, African Americans in

Although African Americans had long been denied the opportunity to compete alongside white athletes, by the 1970s, athletes of African descent had become quite commonplace. Many became role models and heroes of young fans of all races.

In basketball, Julius "Dr. J" Erving (1950–) began his career with the Virginia

Squires of the American Basketball Association (ABA). When the ABA and the National Basketball Association merged in 1976, Erving joined the Philadelphia 76ers, with whom he remained for the next 11 years. Selected as an All-Star in every year of his NBA career, Erving also won the Most Valuable Player in 1981 and led the 76ers to the NBA championship in 1983.

An even greater legend in basketball was Michael "Air" Jordan (1963–). Drafted by the Chicago Bulls after his junior year of college, Jordan earned the nickname "Air" for his ability to leap great distances. In 1991, 1992, and 1993, he led the Bulls to championships. Although he retired before the 1993–1994 season, he returned to basketball prior to the 1995 playoffs. He led his team to the world championship two more times before retiring again in 1998. In 2001, he returned yet again to play for the Washington Wizards.

In football, many of the stars of the past 25 years have been African Americans. One of the game's greatest legends was Walter "Sweetness" Payton (1954–1999) of the NFL's Chicago Bears. In his second season he made the Pro Bowl team for the first of nine times. In 1977, the running back ran a career-high 1,852 yards, helping the Bears reach the playoffs for the first time in 14 years. In 1993, Payton was inducted into the Football Hall of Fame.

In baseball, African Americans have broken many barriers. In 1974, Atlanta Brave Henry Aaron broke Babe Ruth's all-time career home run record by hitting his 715th home run. He would finish his career with a total of 755. In 2001, San Francisco Giant Barry Bonds broke the single season home run record of 70 home runs by hitting 72. In the dugout, Hall of Fame outfielder Frank Robinson broke new ground by becoming the first African American manager in the game's history in 1975.

African American women have also made great strides in sports. In track and

Henry Aaron (Library of Congress)

field, Jackie Joyner-Kersee (1962–) starred at the 1988 Olympics by winning both the hepathlon and the long jump. She won another gold medal in the hepathlon in 1992.

More recently, sisters Venus and Serena Williams (1980– and 1981–) have come to dominate the sport of women's tennis. Venus, who turned pro in 1994 at age 14, won her first singles title in 1998 at the IGA Tennis Classic. She also won the women's singles championship at Wimbleton in 2000. In 1999, Serena won her first career title in the Open Gaz de France. Later that year, Serena became the first African American woman to win the Grand Slam singles title at the U.S. Open since Althea Gibson in 1958.

While African American stars have been relatively rare in professional tennis, they have been even less common in professional golf. However, since 1997, the world's top-ranked golfer has been Tiger Woods, who reached that spot in 1997 at age 21. Since his debut, Woods has won more than 20 championships. Woods, whose father is of mixed African American and white heritage and whose mother is Thai, is both the first African American and the first Asian American to win a major golf championship.

television and film, African Americans in

Although African Americans have been a major influence on American arts and popular culture, the late 20th century saw their influence reach new levels. From television and film, theater and music, African Americans have achieved great success. They have also attracted wide audiences from across all racial lines.

Many of these strides have taken place on television. During the 1970s, Diahann Carroll became the first African American woman to win the lead role in a television series. Her show, "Julia," was about a nurse. Comedian Flip Wilson starred in "The Flip Wilson Show," a variety show that was one of the most popular shows on television for the years 1970 though 1974.

Bill Cosby (*Movie Star News*)

Perhaps the most influential African American comedian and television actor of all time, Bill Cosby was the first African American to win an Emmy Award for Best Actor. In the 1960s, he became the first African American to co-star on a television series, playing a spy on the program *I Spy*. However, Cosby is best known for his groundbreaking 1980s television series *The Cosby Show*, which was the most popular television program in the United States at the time. Since then, Cosby has continued to perform on stage and on television, hosting the program *Kids Say the Darndest Things* (1997–1998), and starring in a second television series, simply called *Cosby* (1996).

In more recent years, many African Americans have started their careers on television and then become major movie stars. Among them are Denzel Washington, who began his career on the medical drama *St. Elsewhere* in the late 1980s before becoming one of film's most respected actors; Eddie Murphy, who starred on *Saturday Night Live* in the early 1980s before becoming a top movie star; Chris Rock, who also had a role on *Saturday Night Live*, in the early 1990s, before moving onto film; and Will Smith, who starred in *The Fresh Prince of Bel Air* in the mid-1990s before starring in such blockbuster films as *Men In Black*. The multi-talented Smith first gained national attention has a rap music star, first as part of the duo the *DJ Jazzy Jeff*, and *Fresh Prince* then as a solo performer.

Another rap star who has added both television and film to her credits is Dana "Queen Latifah" Owens. Queen Latifah has not only had a successful music career, but also starred in the television series *Livin' Single*, hosted her own talk show, and starred in numerous films. In 2003, she was nominated for an Academy Award for her role in the movie musical *Chicago*.

A number of other African American women have achieved great success on television and film. Talk show host Oprah Winfrey began her career at age 19 as the youngest person and the first African American woman to anchor the news at Nashville's WTVF-TV. Two years after moving to Chicago in 1984 to host a morning news program called *A.M. Chicago*, she began her own show, *The Oprah Winfrey Show*. As of 2002, *The Oprah Winfrey Show* has been the top national talk show for 16 straight years. Winfrey's "Oprah's Book Club" segment of the

Spike Lee (*Movie Star News*)

show, in which Winfrey highlighted her favorite recent books, helped make her one of the most influential people in America, since books that were featured by the club often became bestsellers. As of 2002, Winfrey ranked as the highest paid woman in the United States.

In recent years, a number of African Americans have also gained fame from behind the movie camera as directors. Perhaps the best known is Spike Lee. In 1986, he won the Best New Director Award at the Cannes Film Festival. Since then, he has created many feature films and documentaries that present views of African American culture and race relations. Among his best-known works is the controversial *Do the Right Thing*. This earned him an Academy award nomination for Best Original Screenplay in 1989. More recent films have included **Malcolm X** (see p. 87), a biography of the **Nation of Islam** leader (see p. 61); *Get On the Bus*, about a group of African American men on a bus trip to Washington, D.C. to participate in the **Million Man March** (see p. 117); and the documentary, *Four Little Girls*, about the **Birmingham, Alabama** (see p. 77) bomb explosion that killed four African American girls during their Sunday School class in 1963.

In addition to Lee, other well-known black directors in recent years include John Singleton, director of *Boyz N the Hood*, a film about life in South Central Los Angeles.

Thomas, Clarence

Clarence Thomas was born in rural Georgia in 1948 and raised by his grandparents. After attending Holy Cross University and Yale University Law School, he was appointed by President Ronald Reagan to head the Equal Employment Opportunity Commission (EEOC). In 1989, President George H. W. Bush appointed Thomas to the U.S. Board of Appeals and then to the

U.S. Supreme Court. Thomas, who is only the second African American to serve on the Supreme Court (see **Thurgood Marshall**, p. 89), is one of the more conservative members of the Court. He has opposed **affirmative action** (see p. 105) and other programs that use race as a means of determining government assistance.

Glossary

boycott: to refuse to buy, sell, or use.

clergymen: people ordained for religious services, such as a minister, priest, or rabbi.

deported: to be sent away, or forced to leave the country by official government order.

doctorate: the highest level of graduate degree offered by a university.

electoral votes: a group elected by voters to perform the formal duty of electing the president of the United States. Each state is represented by the same number of representatives that it has in Congress. Each state's electors are expected to cast their votes for the candidate selected by the popular vote in their state. Usually, the candidate that wins the highest number of popular votes nationwide wins enough electoral votes to become president, although not always. In both the 1876 election and the 2000 election, the candidate with the most popular votes nationally lost the election.

executive order: a policy issued by the president that does not require approval from Congress.

exodus: a departure by a large group. The term usually refers to the exodus of the Jews out of Egypt as told in the Bible.

folklore: the unwritten beliefs, traditions, stories, legends, and customs of a people, passed from one generation to the next.

grandfather clause: a law passed in many areas of the South to prevent African Americans from voting. According to the grandfather clause, only those whose grandfathers could legally vote were allowed to vote. This prevented many African Americans from going to the polls since their grandparents were often enslaved.

nonviolent resistance: a form of civil disobedience promoted by Dr. Martin Luther King, Jr. in which protesters refrain from violence or physical force. Dr. King was influenced by the teaching of Mohandas K. Gandhi, a leader of a struggle against British control of India in the early 20th century.

poll tax: a form of preventing African Americans to vote. Many southern communities passed poll-tax laws, which required voters to pay a tax in order to vote. This prevented many African Americans who could not afford to pay the tax from voting.

propaganda: the spreading of information for the purpose of promoting one's cause or beliefs, or to damage the cause or beliefs of one's opponent.

secede: to withdraw from or seperate from, such as the states of the Confederacy seceding from the United States during the Civil War.

segregation: the seperation of one racial or other group from the majority of society.

separatist: a person who promotes withdrawing or seceding from the larger group. Black separatists, for example, promoted cutting ties to the white majority.

settlement house: an institution usually located in a poor community that offers social services as well as educational and recreation activities.

suffrage: the right to vote in elections.

tenant farmer: a person who farms land owned by another person and pays rent in cash or in a share of the crops; a sharecropper.

theology: the study of religion.

trusts: a combination of businesses in which a single group of managers controls a market either by buying all competitors or running them out of business. Trusts are now illegal in the United States.

Tuskegee Airmen: an all-black group of pilots trained at the Tuskagee Institute in Alabama during World War II. The pilots that served as part of the group were among the most highly decorated members of the U.S. Armed forces. Not a single plane flown by the group was shot down by enemy fire during 1944 or 1945 when the group was flying missions in Europe.

Resources

General Subjects

BOOKS

Abdul-Jabbar, Kareem, and Alan Steingberg. *Black Profiles in Courage: A Legacy of African-American Achievement*. New York: Morrow, 1996.

Altman, Susan. *Encyclopedia of African American Heritage*. 1st Edition. New York: Facts on File, 2001.

Bell, Janet Cheatham. *Stretch Your Wings: Famous Black Quotations for Teens*. New York: Little, Brown & Company, 1999.

Christian, Charles M. and Sari J. Bennett. *Black Saga—The African American Experience: A Chronology*. Baltimore, MD: Counterpoint Press, 1998.

Haber, Louis. *Black Pioneers of Science and Invention*. New York: Harcourt, Brace, & World Inc., 1970.

Hancock, Sibyl. *Famous Firsts of Black Americans*. Gretna, LA: Pelican, 1983.

Hine, Darlene C., and Kathleen Thompson. *Facts on File Encyclopedia of Black Women in America*. New York: Facts on File, 1997.

Hudson, Wade. *Book of Black Heroes: From A to Z: Volume One*. East Orange, NJ: Just Us Books, 1988.

Karenga, Maulana. *Kwanzaa: A Celebration of Family, Community and Culture*. Los Angeles: University of Sankore Press, 1997.

Kranz, Rachel. *The Biographical Dictionary of Black Americans*. New York: Facts of File, 1992.

Myers, Walter Dean. *Now Is Your Time: The African American Struggle for Freedom*. New York: HarperCollins, 1992.

New York Public Library African American Desk Reference. Schomburg Center for Research in Black Culture. New York: Wiley, 1999.

New York Public Library Amazing African American History: A Book of Answers for Kids. New York: Wiley, 1997.

Pinkney, Andrea Davis. *Let It Shine: Stories of Black Women Freedom Fighters*. New York: Harcourt, 2000.

Richardson, Ben Albert. *Great Black Americans*. 2d rev. ed. New York: Crowell, 1976.

Smith, Jesse Carne, ed. *Notable Black American Women*. Third Edition. Detroit, MI: Gale, 2002.

Stewart, Jeffrey C. *1001 Things Everyone Should Know About African American History*. New York: Doubleday, 1997.

Turner, Glennette Tilley. *Follow in Their Footsteps*. New York: Cobblehill Books, 1997.

Yarbrough, Camille. *Cornrows*. New York: Paper Star, 1997.

Audio

Every Tone a Testimony: A Smithsonian Folkways African American Aural History. Washington, DC: Smithsonian Folkways Recordings, 2001.

The Long Road to Freedom: An Anthology of Black Music. New York: Buddah, 2001.

Our Souls Have Grown Deep Like the Rivers: Black Poets Read Their Work. Westwood, CA: WEA/Rhino, 2000.

CD-ROM

Encarta Africana Library of Black America. 3rd. ed. Redmond, WA: Microsoft, 2000.

WEBSITES

Africa Online–Africa Kids Only: http://www.africaonline.com/site/africa/kids.jsp

African American History and Culture: http://www.si.edu/resource/faq/nmah/afroam.htm

The African American Journey: http://www2.worldbook.com/students/feature_index.asp

African American Mosaic: http://lcweb.loc.gov/exhibits/african/afam001.html

African American Oddysey: http://memory.loc.gov/ammem/aaohtml/aohome.html

AFROAmeric@ Kid's Zone: http://www.afro.com/kidstalk/

AFRO-American Almanac: http://www.toptags.com/aama/index.htm

Anacostia Museum and Center for African American History and Culture: http://anacostia.si.edu/

Education First Black History Activities: http://www.kn.pacbell.com/wired/BHM/AfroAm.html

Lest We Forget: http://www.coax.net/people/lwf/

National Civil Rights Museum: http://www.civilrightsmuseum.org/

History and Biography

(Since 1876)

BOOKS

Bond, Julian, ed. *Lift Every Voice and Sing: A Celebration of the Negro National Anthem: 100 Years, 100 Voices*. New York: Random House, 2000.

Fireside, Harvey. *Brown v. Board of Education: Equal Schooling For All.* Hillside, NJ: Enslow, 1994.

Haskins, James. *The March On Washington.* New York: HarperCollins, 1993.

Katz, William Loren. *Black People Who Made The Old West.* New York: Facts on File, 1992.

Lawrence, Jacob. *The Great Migration.* New York: HarperCollins, 1993.

Pinkney, Andrea Davis. *Alvin Ailey.* New York: Hyperion, 1995.

Thomas, Velma Maia. *Freedom's Children: The Passage from Emancipation to the Great Migration.* New York: Crown Publishers, 2000.

VIDEO

Black Americans of Achievement: Alice Walker. Wynnewood, PA: Schlesinger Media, 1992.

Black Americans of Achievement: Booker T. Washington. Wynnewood, PA: Schlesinger Media, 1992.

Black Americans of Achievement: Colin Powell. Wynnewood, PA: Schlesinger Media, 1992.

Black Americans of Achievement: Elijah Muhammad. Wynnewood, PA: Schlesinger Media, 1992.

Black Americans of Achievement: George Washington Carver. Wynnewood, PA: Schlesinger Media, 1992.

Black Americans of Achievement: James Baldwin. Wynnewood, PA: Schlesinger Media, 1992.

Black Americans of Achievement: Jesse Jackson. Wynnewood, PA: Schlesinger Media, 1992.

Black Americans of Achievement: Jesse Owens. Wynnewood, PA: Schlesinger Media, 1992.

Black Americans of Achievement: Langston Hughes. Wynnewood, PA: Schlesinger Media, 1992.

Black Americans of Achievement: Malcolm X. Wynnewood, PA: Schlesinger Media, 1992.

Black Americans of Achievement: Marcus Garvey. Wynnewood, PA: Schlesinger Media, 1992.

Black Americans of Achievement: Martin Luther King, Jr. Wynnewood, PA: Schlesinger Media, 1992.

Black Americans of Achievement: Mary McLeod Bethune. Wynnewood, PA: Schlesinger Media, 1992.

Black Americans of Achievement: Matthew Henson. Wynnewood, PA: Schlesinger Media, 1992.

Black Americans of Achievement: Muhammad Ali. Wynnewood, PA: Schlesinger Media, 1992.

Black Americans of Achievement: Thurgood Marshall. Wynnewood, PA: Schlesinger Media, 1992.

Black Americans of Achievement: W.E.B. Du Bois. Wynnewood, PA: Schlesinger Media, 1992.

WEBSITES
Buffalo Soldiers on the Western Frontier: http://www.imh.org/imh/buf/buftoc.html

Harlem: 1900–1940: An African American Community: http://www.si.umich.edu/CHICO/Harlem/

Harlem Renaissance: http://www.bigchalk.com/cgi-bin/WebObjects/WOPortal.woa/Homework/ Elementary/Literature/ Literature_by_Culture/Reading_About_African- American_Life/Harlem_Renaissance_21247.html

Jackie Robinson and Other Baseball Highlights:
http://memory.loc.gov/ammem/jrhtml/jrhome.html

Martin Luther King, Jr. and the Civil Rights Movement:
http://seattletimes.nwsource.com/mlk/index.html

Timeline of the American Civil Rights Movement: http://www.wmich.edu/politics/mlk/
Tuskegee Airmen: http://tuskegeeairmen.org/

AUDIO
Martin Luther King, Jr. Tapes. CD. Soundworks, 1994.

Folklore, Fiction, and Poetry

BOOKS
Hamilton, Virginia. *The People Could Fly: The Book of Black Folktales.* New York: Random House, 2000.

Hudson, Wade, and Cheryl Willis Hudson. *In Praise of Our Fathers and Our Mothers: A Black Family Treasury by Outstanding Authors and Artists.* East Orange, NJ: Just Us Books, 1997.

Hughes, Langston. *The Block: Poems.* New York: Viking, 1995.

Lester, Julius. *The Tales of Uncle Remus: The Adventures of B'rer Rabbit.* New York: Puffin, 1999.

McKissock, Pat. *The Dark-Thirty: Southern Tales of the Supernatural.* New York: Knopf, 1996.

Myers, Walter Dean. *Monster.* New York: Harper Collins, 1999.

Rollins, Charlemae Hill, ed. *Christmas Gif': An Anthology of Christmas Poems, Songs, and Stories Written by and About African-Americans.* New York: Morrow Junior Books, 1993.

Selected Bibliography

Andrews, William L., and Henry Lewis Gates Jr. *Slave Narratives*. New York: Library of America, 2000.

Appiah, Kwame Anthony, and Henry Lewis Gates Jr. *Africana: The Encyclopedia of the African and African American Experience*. New York: Basic Civitas Books, 1999.

Barbeau, Arthur, and Florette Henri. *The Unknown Soldiers: African American Troops in World War I*. New York: Da Capo, 1996.

Bennett, Lerone, Jr. *Pioneers in Protest*. Chicago: Johnson Publishing, 1968.

Berlin, Ira. *Many Thousands Gone: The First Two Centuries of Slavery in North America*. Cambridge, MA: Harvard University Press, 2000.

Branch, Taylor. *Parting the Waters*. New York: Simon & Schuster, 1989.

———. *Pillar of Fire*. New York: Simon & Schuster, 1998.

Cowan, Tom, and Jack Maguire. *Timelines of African-American History: Five Hundred Years of Black Achievement*. New York: Berkley Publishing Group, 1994.

DjeDje, Jacqueline Cogdell. *Turn Up the Volume!: A Celebration of African Music*. Berkeley: University of California Press, 1998.

Dodd, Donald. *Historical Statistics of the United States*. Westport, CT: Greenwood Publishing Group, Inc., 1993.

Du Bois, W. E. B. *Souls of Black Folk*. New York: NAL/Dutton, 1995.

Finkelman, Paul. *Slavery in the Courtroom: An Annotated Bibliography of American Cases.* Washington: Lawbook Exchange, 1996.

Foner, Eric. *Reconstruction.* New York: HarperCollins, 1989.

Garrow, David. *Bearing the Cross: Martin Luther King, Jr. and the Southern Christian Leadership Conference, 1955–1968.* New York: William Morrow, 1999.

Harley, Sharon. *The Timetables of African-American History.* New York: Simon & Schuster, 1995.

Hughes, Langston, et al. *A Pictorial History of African Americans*, 6th ed. New York: Crown Publishing, 1995.

Kelley, Robin D. G., and Earl Lewis. *To Make Ourselves Anew: A History of African Americans.* New York: Oxford University Press, 2000.

McPherson, James. *Ordeal by Fire: The Civil War and Reconstruction.* New York: Knopf, 1992.

Peterson, Robert W. *Only the Ball Was White.* Oxford: Oxford University Press, 1992.

Ploski, Harry, and James Williams, eds. *Encyclopedia of African-American History.* New York: Macmillan Library Reference USA, 1996.

Schubert, Frank. *Black Valor: Buffalo Soldiers and the Medal of Honor, 1870–1898.* Wilmington, DE: Scholarly Resources, 1997.

Smith, Carter, ed. *The Black Experience.* New York: Facts On File, Inc., 1990.

Thomas, Velma Maia. *Freedom's Children: The Passage from Emancipation to the Great Migration.* New York: Crown Publishing, 2000.

U.S. Census Bureau. Annual Yearbook. Washington, DC: Government Printing Office, 1996.

——. Reports. Washington, DC: Government Printing Office, 1900, 1910, 1920, 1930, 1940, 1950.

Index

Note: The index below contains entries for both volumes of the Student Almanac *of African American History. The roman numeral I refers to pages in the first volume. The roman numeral II refers to pages in the second volume.*

84, 92, 95, 115, 118
sports, African Americans in, **II:** 30,
93, 120
Stevens, Thaddeus, **I:** 101, 124, 125
Stono rebellion, **I:** 40
Strauder v. *West Virginia*, **II:** 14, 30
Student Nonviolent Coordinating
Committee (SNCC), **II:** 72, 73, 80,
92, 93, 95, 96

T

television and film, African Americans
in, **II:** 102, 104, 122
Terrell, Mary Church, **II:** 31
Thomas, Clarence, **II:** 101, 103, 124
triangle trade, **I:** 14, 30,34
Truth, Sojourner, **I:** 10, 68, 69, 89
Tubman, Harriet, **I:** 10, 70, 71, 89,
90, 99
Tulsa Riot, **II:** 41, 66
Turner, Nat, **I:** 66, 67, 90
Tuskegee Institute, **II:** 14, 17, 31, 38

U

U.S. Constitution, **I:** 9, 43, 56, 62, 106
U.S. Civil War **I:** 8, 10, 108; **II:** 13,
16, 26, 28, 32

Uncle Tom's Cabin, **I:** 90
Underground Railroad, **I:** 67, 76, 79,
90, 91, 99
United States v. *Cruikshank*, **I:** 104,
125

V

Vesey Conspiracy, **I:** 66, 92
Virginia House of Burgesses, **I:** 35
Voting Rights Act of 1965, **II:** 74, 95

W

Walker, David, **I:** 66, 93
Wallace, George, **II:** 76, 96
War of 1812, **I:** 9, 43, 56, 62
Washington, Booker T., **II:** 14, 17, 32,
38, 48, 51, 63
Wells, Ida B., **II:** 17, 34
West Indies, **I:** 14, 35, 54, 55
Wheatley, Phillis, **I:** 39, 63
World War I, **II:** 9, 39, 40, 55, 57, 67
World War II, **II:** 9, 43, 44, 52, 55,
56, 57, 67, 69